Home Security

THE COMPLETE HANDBOOK

CALVIN BECKFORD
AND
HEATHER ALSTON

NH
NEW
HOLLAND

DEDICATION

Peter Beckford, Master Builder

First published in 2005 by New Holland Publishers (UK) Ltd
Garfield House, 86–88 Edgware Road
London W2 2EA
United Kingdom
London • Cape Town • Sydney • Auckland
www.newhollandpublishers.com

Copyright © 2005 text Calvin Beckford and Heather Alston
Copyright © 2005 illustrations New Holland Publishers (UK) Ltd
Copyright © 2005 New Holland Publishers (UK) Ltd

1 3 5 7 9 10 8 6 4 2

ISBN 1 84330 911 4

Senior Editor: Corinne Masciocchi
Main Illustrator: Sue Rose
Designer: e Design Associates
DIY projects illustrations and cover photograph: AG&G Books

Printed and bound by Kyodo Printing Co (Singapore) Pte Ltd

DECLARATION

The views expressed in this book are those of the authors
and do not necessarily reflect those of her and her employers.

The publishers have made every effort to ensure that the information contained
in this book is correct at the time of going to press. All recommendations are made
without guarantee on the part of the authors and the publishers. The authors and publishers
disclaim any liability for damages or injury resulting from use of this information.

Secured by Design is a security initiative owned by the Association of Chief Police Officers.
It establishes levels of security for buildings and correction of environmental features
that affect crime. The title and logo are Registered Trademarks and may only be used
by the Police service or under licence by companies whose products have met
the standards nominated by the project. This publication is endorsed by
Secured by Design as supporting the principles of the project.

See www.securedbydesign.com or contact ACPO CPI Ltd on 0207 227 3423

Contents

Foreword

Everyone wants to protect their home from the threat of burglary as best as they can, but unfortunately too many households have to experience the loss and distress of being burgled. Most burglaries are committed by opportunist thieves, so with a few simple measures, home owners can help deter thieves from targeting their home.

There are numerous sources of conflicting advice and information on crime prevention available to home owners and sometimes these are provided by organisations or companies with limited knowledge and experience of crime prevention. It is therefore understandable that many people either fail to appreciate the importance of such measures or feel overwhelmed by the variety and technical content of advice and information available.

It is therefore refreshing to come across a book that provides simple but effective advice to home owners and is compiled by people with first-hand knowledge and experience of crime prevention. *Home Security* is written in an easy-to-understand and informative style that offers simple and cost-effective measures to help all householders interested in maximising the protection of their homes and neighbourhoods. The advice and information include low-cost, low-maintenance measures to safeguard your home both inside and out.

Home Security is a practical, well researched guide using straightforward, concise language. The security measures described here are easy and inexpensive to effectuate and will greatly contribute towards minimising the risk of burglary and making your home a safer place.

Nigel Davies
Director
National Neighbourhood Watch Association

Assessing the risk

Many people are concerned that they, or their relatives or friends, may become victims of crime, and the most common concerns are burglary, car theft, mugging and physical attack. The good news, though, is that in 2004 the British Crime Survey announced that the risk of anyone becoming the victim of a crime in any one year has been falling and now stands at 27 per cent, which is about the same as it was in 1981.

Of course, the problem with such statistics, or at least the information extracted from them that appears in newspapers and on television, is that the figures are very general and won't necessarily tell you anything about what's going on in your street or your village. The burglary rates in England and Wales may well have fallen by around 40 per cent over the past six years but the fact remains that crime concerns and affects everyone in very different ways, depending on where they live, their age, their wealth, their gender and their racial origin.

The aim of this book is to help you protect your home from burglary and theft, and the good news about this is that crime prevention measures do actually work. Research has proved that those who apply the crime prevention techniques described in this book and advised by the police and security companies stand considerably less chance of being burgled. And buying your security (apart from intruder alarms, which require regular maintenance) is a one-off cost that will pay dividends for as long as you live in that house or flat – which is money worth spending.

Apart from security devices, there are other factors that make a difference to your chances of being burgled. Occupancy is a key factor, because most burglars don't want to be seen or disturbed by a householder or a neighbour. Where you live makes a difference, too. People whose homes are in inner cities have a greater risk of being burgled than someone living in the suburbs, while those in detached houses have a higher risk of burglary than their flat-dwelling neighbours. But again, these figures are based on a nationwide survey, and you shouldn't fall into the trap of believing that just because you live in a flat, you're safer. There may well be local anomalies that buck the trend.

Burglary doesn't occur at regular intervals throughout the day; it mirrors the lifestyle of the burglar. The quiet time for burglary is the morning, but it increases gradually as the day progresses, reaching a peak in the evening. About a quarter of burglaries happen between midnight and six o'clock in the morning but there will be local variations, however. Some police areas see an increase in crime in the autumn, when the nights start drawing in and it becomes easier to see who's in and who's out by the lack of lights showing, whereas others experience peaks in July and August, when people are away on holiday, leaving homes unoccupied.

Clearly, there are a lot of factors at play, which make it difficult to assess the likelihood of being burgled. What is not difficult, however, is doing something to reduce the risk to an absolute minimum. Not everyone is burgled; in fact, at the

A few myths about burglars

Before getting into risk assessment, it's worth dispelling a number of myths about burglars, because the majority are not as clever as you may think.

Myth *Burglars can pick locks.*
Fact Unless a burglar is a skilled locksmith with a wide range of lock picking devices, and is prepared to spend considerable time outside your front or back door, manipulating levers and pins through the keyholes, it is extremely unlikely that picking a lock will be the chosen method of entry. Most burglars will simply kick the door in or smash glass to reach a key left in a lock.

Myth *It is clear that my burglary was planned, because they knew what time I left for work.*
Fact Just over 80 per cent of burglaries occur when there is nobody at home, but the vast majority are not planned. To discover if you're at home during the day, some burglars will simply knock on the door, having a ready excuse for calling if someone should answer.

Myth *The burglar slipped the lock with a credit card.*
Fact This method of entry through a front door can only be used on the sort of rounded bolt you find on an ordinary night latch. Even then, the door has to be loose fitting so that the plastic can be bent around the doorstop. In reality, if your door can be opened with a piece of plastic, it's a very insecure door, and you should do something about it.

Myth *Most burglars carry keys.*
Fact There are many lock manufacturers producing hundreds of different locks, requiring millions of different

keys. An ordinary British Standard 3621 mortice deadlock will have at least a thousand key differs, so the burglar would be wasting his time by carrying bunches of house keys – unless, of course, you've only got a two-lever lock on your back door, for which there will only be about 20 different keys.

Myth *Most burglars go 'tooled up' to break into a house.*
Fact Carrying house breaking implements with the intention to steal is an offence in itself, and a burglar risks arrest if stopped by the police. To get around this problem, a burglar tends to carry only one or two tools, such as a screwdriver or a chisel, with which to break through a poorly secured door or window. If they need other tools, they will usually find them in your garden or a poorly secured shed. A garden spade, with its cutting edge, makes an ideal lever for forcing open doors and windows. Make sure you lock these items away at all times.

Myth *There was so little mess in my house that the burglars must have been professionals.*
Fact Most burglars cause the minimum amount of damage at the entry point, and only as much mess as is necessary to find the things they want to steal, such as jewellery, cash, credit cards and portable electrical items. Wanton damage, such as graffiti and torn furniture, is uncommon. They simply don't have the time to hang around – by the way, burglary is not a profession!

Myth *The burglar was so clever that he broke in without leaving any sign of forcing.*
Fact It is most likely that the intruder found a door or window open.

time of writing, fewer than 4 per cent of households had suffered one or more burglaries or attempts each year.

For a burglary to take place, three conditions must be satisfied:

● there must be a suitable target (the contents of your home);

● the absence of a capable guardian (a person, an alarm or good locks);

● the presence of a likely offender.

Modifying any one of these conditions will prevent the burglary from occurring.

You can do something about any potential target by locking it away in a safe, or perhaps taking it with you when you go out. If you can't do that, you may be able to make it less attractive to a thief by ensuring that it is identifiable with a security postcode (see p 126).

You can't do much about the offender, so you'll have to rely on the police to remove him from the equation.

However, you can do something about the absence of a capable guardian, by putting up better fences, installing an alarm, fitting window locks, improving your security lighting and making a myriad other physical improvements that not only reduce the risk of burglary, but also will help you to feel safer.

So welcome to this home security guide, where you'll find the information you need to protect your property. Remember, however, that you can always obtain more advice from the crime prevention department of your local police station, and if you have any new ideas for crime prevention, the authors would be pleased to receive your email (see the bottom of p 176 for further details).

If you're interested in finding out more about burglary, visit the British Crime Survey website, while for crime prevention techniques and help in carrying out a risk assessment of your home, visit the Home Office crime reduction website (see Useful Contacts, p 12). If you don't have access to the internet at home, try your local library or visit an internet café.

Home security risk assessment

Now that a few of the myths have been dispelled, you can carry out a full risk assessment of your home, using the checklists provided. A few questions concerning your safety in the home have also been included, because when you're at home, your safety must take priority over security. It's a good idea for two people to carry out the assessment, so that as you work your way through the list, you can bounce ideas off each other and one of you can record the weak points. Some suggest that you consider how you might get in if you were to lock yourself out, but this ignores the fact that burglars would rather not be seen, whereas you wouldn't care, so you could actually overestimate your security needs. It is better to imagine yourself as a burglar, someone who is concerned about being discovered and arrested. The purpose of the checklists is to get you thinking about security; once you've made a list of your home's weaknesses, you can turn to the relevant pages to see what can be done about them.

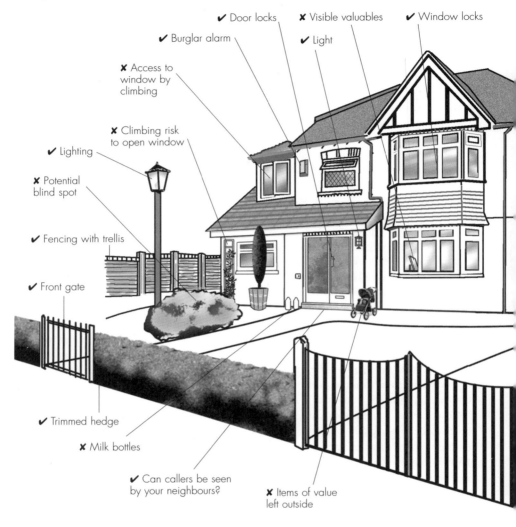

✔ Door locks   ✘ Visible valuables   ✔ Window locks

✔ Burglar alarm   ✔ Light

✘ Access to window by climbing

✘ Climbing risk to open window

✔ Lighting

✘ Potential blind spot

✔ Fencing with trellis

✔ Front gate

✔ Trimmed hedge

✘ Milk bottles

✔ Can callers be seen by your neighbours?

✘ Items of value left outside

Security issues around the home

It would be difficult to write checklists for every type of home, and you may find that some do not apply to your specific situation. However, all the relevant areas of concern have been covered and this book should guide you in the right direction.

Risk assessment checklist
THE FRONT GARDEN OR HARD STANDING

● Do the shrubs in the garden obscure the front of the house or flat and provide cover for a burglar to operate?

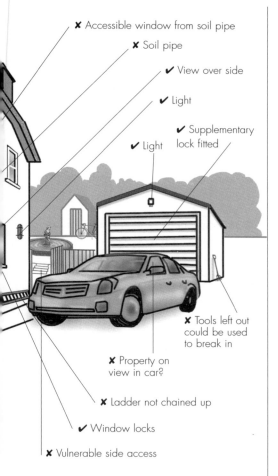

✗ Accessible window from soil pipe

✗ Soil pipe

✔ View over side

✔ Light

✔ Supplementary lock fitted

✔ Light

✗ Tools left out could be used to break in

✗ Property on view in car?

✗ Ladder not chained up

✔ Window locks

✗ Vulnerable side access

KEY
✗ = security risk
✔ = good security feature

● Are there items in the garden that could be used to force open an entrance door or break glass?

● Are there items of value in the front garden that can be easily stolen?

● Are there items or features in the garden that can be climbed to gain access to upper windows and balconies?

● As you approach the entrance door, are there any blind spots where someone could hide?

● Can callers at the door be seen by your neighbours and from the street?

● Where is the spare front-door key? Under a flowerpot or the doormat?

● If you do not park your car in a locked garage, are there items of value on view in your car?

● Do you have a front gate?

☽ After dark
● Is there a light in the front garden?

● Does the light cast any dark shadows that could provide cover for a burglar to operate?

● Do fitted lights work?

THE FRONT OF YOUR HOME
● If you have an intruder alarm, can the bell box be seen from the road?

● Are there items of value on view in the windows?

● Are any of the first-floor windows accessible by climbing?

● Is the entrance door deeply recessed?

9

- Is it possible to see if the mail or a newspaper has been delivered?

- If milk or bread is delivered when you are out, where is it left?

- If your basement flat is reached from the front of the building, are the steps gated and secured at street level?

- If you have an integral garage, do you use and rely on the factory fitted garage door lock?

- Is the communal entrance door to your block of flats fitted with an access controlled lock?

- Does your access controlled entrance door have a tradesman's button, and what are the hours of operation?

- Are your ground-floor windows, and those that are accessible by climbing, in good condition and fitted with sufficient locks of the right type, in the right positions to resist a burglar?

- Are your doors in good condition and do they have locks of the right type, in the right positions to resist a burglar?

After dark

- Is there a light outside the entrance door?

- Does the light illuminate the face of a caller at the door, or does it place the caller's face in shadow?

- Does the light come on automatically when you are away?

- Is the house or flat number, or house or block of flats name, clearly visible from the street so that the emergency services can find you easily?

- Do you leave any windows open for ventilation at night?

- Do fitted lights work?

THE SIDE OF YOUR HOME

- Can you easily walk along the side of the building?

- Having walked along the side of the building, can you be seen from the street?

- Are any of the first-floor windows accessible by climbing such features as cast-iron soil pipes?

- Is there a lockable gate at the entrance to the side drive or path in line with the front of the building?

- If your garage is at the side of the house, do you use and rely on the factory fitted garage door lock?

- Can you climb over the garage roof into the back garden?

- Can you look over the side drive from indoors through a ground-floor or upper window?

- Is there a water tap on the side wall of the building?

- Are your ground-floor windows, and those that are accessible by climbing, in good condition and fitted with sufficient window locks of the right type and in the right positions to resist a burglar?

● Are your doors in good condition and do they have locks of the right type, in the right positions to resist a burglar?

☾ After dark
● Is the side of the building illuminated at night?

● Do fitted lights work?

● Can your parked vehicle be used to aid climbing over a fence, wall or gate?

● Do you leave any windows open for ventilation at night?

THE BACK GARDEN
● Are the perimeter fences or walls easy to climb?

● Is it easy for an intruder to get into your garden from a neighbour's garden?

● Is there open land, an open alleyway or a service road behind your home?

● If your garage is reached by means of a rear service road, do you use and rely on the factory fitted garage door lock?

● Is there an unsecured ladder in your back garden or the garden of a neighbour?

● Is the garden shed door fitted with a substantial lock?

● Do you leave garden tools outside?

● Are there garden tools in an insecure greenhouse or other outbuilding?

● Are there items of value in the garden?

● Is the access gate into your garden difficult to climb and securely locked?

● Does someone water the plants and cut the grass when you go away?

☾ After dark
● Is the back garden illuminated at night?

● Does the light come on automatically when you are away?

● Do you have lights that are triggered by movement in the garden?

● Do fitted lights work?

● Can you see most of your garden from an upstairs window at night?

THE BACK OF YOUR HOME
● If you have an intruder alarm, can the bell box be seen from the end of your garden?

● Are there items of value on view in the windows?

● Are any of the first-floor windows accessible by climbing?

● Are your doors in good condition and do they have locks of the right type, in the right positions to resist a burglar?

11

- Are your ground-floor windows, and those that are accessible by climbing, in good condition and fitted with sufficient window locks of the right type, in the right positions to resist a burglar?

After dark

- Are there lights outside the back doors?

- Do the back-door lights come on automatically when you are away?

- Do fitted lights work?

- Do you leave any windows open for ventilation at night?

INDOORS

- Do you have a plan in the event of a fire? – Get out, stay out and dial 999.

- Have your gas appliances (cooker, heater, boiler) been serviced recently?

- Are you overloading your electrical sockets?

- Do you smoke in bed?

- Can you hear if anyone walks up to the front of your home?

- Can you hear close approaches to your windows on the ground floor?

- Have you marked your property with your postcode and house or flat number?

- Do you have a safe?

- Is there an intruder alarm?

- Do you have smoke and carbon monoxide detectors?

- Do you leave cash or credit cards lying about?

- Where do you keep your spare keys?

- Do you have contents insurance, and is the cover sufficient?

After dark

- Do some of the house lights come on automatically when you are out or away on holiday?

- Do you key lock yourself in at night?

USEFUL CONTACTS
British Crime Survey
www.homeoffice.gov.uk/rds/bcs1.html

Home Office Crime Reduction Centre
www.crimereduction.gov.uk

Secured by Design
www.securedbydesign.com

CHAPTER 1

Boundaries

Most of our homes will have something that marks the boundary of our property. This could be a physical barrier, such as a fence or wall, or a simple indicator created by coloured paving or a strip of landscaping. We like to have control over the space around our homes, so we create thresholds or psychological markers. For example, a low brick wall and gate at the front of a house are recognisable features. They can be climbed over without difficulty, but reinforce the message that the space behind the wall is private.

We tend to use solid structures, such as walls, railings and wooden fences, to mark our boundaries. In addition, a well maintained wall or fence will enhance the general appearance of your property. A crumbling wall or a broken fence also makes a statement, but one that suggests that the rest of the house may be in need of maintenance; but more importantly, such a boundary could provide an access opportunity for a burglar.

Easy access to buildings is essential. A footpath to a front door must be functional, allowing us to get from the street to the door without getting covered in mud or injuring ourselves. In the majority of cases, a path or driveway has a decorative purpose as well. The boundary and footpath are normally the first parts of the property a visitor sees; they will also be noticed by the opportunist burglar.

The design and layout of a footpath can enhance the security of your home, or hinder it. Many of us will have inherited a concrete path that leads in a straight line from the street to the front door, or perhaps across the front of the house to the door. While concrete can look austere, it is a practical and hardwearing material. More importantly, however, the layout of such a pathway ensures that it is in full view of the house, allowing you to see callers approaching the property.

With the growing interest in garden make-overs, some home owners have created more informal layouts with curving paths and borders of mixed shrubs that make a more pleasing picture. In most cases, however, home security has not been considered, and very often the attractively designed garden creates opportunities for the burglar, such as places to hide and plants or ornaments to steal. Although there may be constraints in terms of safety or design, when planning a garden make-over, consider using gravel for pathways. It is impossible to walk on gravel without making a noise, which will allow you to hear anyone approaching. When planting shrubs next to a footpath, make sure that they will not grow so high as to obscure the view. As a general rule, footpaths should be clearly visible from inside your home.

Often, however, your first line of defence against a burglar is a fence or a side gate, so they must be high enough and strong enough to deter the casual intruder. An ordinary 1.8-m (6-ft) fence or wall will not put off the determined thief.

If you are concerned about the security of your home's boundaries, this chapter will show you how you can improve them to cope with any normal risk. If you think you need a higher level of protection, consult your local fencing professionals.

Security issues for walls and fences

● Normally, a fence or wall at the front of a property facing a street should be around 1 m (3 ft) high, and ideally no higher than 1.2 m (4 ft). This allows passers-by to look into the garden, preventing a would-be intruder from approaching the house unseen. If you want a higher front fence or wall, you'll need planning permission for any structure above 1 m (3 ft) if it abuts the highway. Contact your local planning department before undertaking any work.

● If trees and shrubs form part of the front boundary, make sure there are generous gaps between them so that no one can hide behind them. Large overgrown shrubs in the front garden could provide cover for a burglar, allowing him to force open a window unseen from the street or houses opposite.

● A standard 1.8-m (6-ft) high fence or wall in the back garden is sufficient provided there is no public access to it. If there is an alleyway, a railway line or open land on the other side of the fence, increase its height to at least 2 m (6 ft 6 in) and add 300–600 mm (1–2 ft) of trellis on top.

● Fences at the back of the property that are higher than 2 m (6 ft 6 in) require planning permission, but check with your local planning department to see if they would allow you to add a small trellis topping without having to make a planning application.

● Divisional fencing between gardens should at least deter the 'fence hopping' burglar, who gets into one garden and then climbs over a fence to reach the house he wants to burgle.

● If you have moved into a new home and all there is between you and your neighbour is a simple post-and-wire fence, you should replace it immediately, perhaps with a trellis and panel fence. Although a wire fence will allow you to see anyone beyond your property, it will provide no protection at all at night.

● A fence should have a long life, so always choose pressure-treated (tanalised) timber. Brush preservative on to any bare patches or cuts; it's a good idea to soak the ends of timber posts in a bucket of preservative before setting them in concrete or fitting them to post spikes.

● To prevent anyone from sitting on your front garden wall, consider topping it with a low railing, positioned towards the outer edge.

● If your boundary wall attracts graffiti, clean it off and apply an anti-graffiti glaze to make future removal easier. If you don't like the shiny finish of the glaze, try using a matt sacrificial coating, which you can wash off with the graffiti using hot water. You'll then have to treat the surface again with the sacrificial coating. Leaving graffiti in place will simply encourage more; removing it as soon as you see it will deter others from using your wall as a canvas. Anti-graffiti products can be obtained from locksmiths and some DIY stores.

- A wall or fence can be protected from graffiti if you grow a climbing shrub on it. If there's a problem with loitering, you can plant a thorny variety, but you may have to erect a temporary fence to protect the plants while they mature.

- If your property borders accessible open land, consider growing thorny plants on either side of your fence and over the top (*see Chap 10*). You should obtain permission first to grow plants on the land outside your property.

Types of wooden fencing

Certain types of fencing are more robust than others when it comes to creating a long lasting, protective boundary. Wooden fences are not the best means of keeping out intruders, but they will deter the

climbing burglar, or at least make it more difficult for him to get in and out, which may be enough to make him think again. The primary role of the wooden fence is to provide a degree of privacy and shelter in the garden.

FENCING PANELS

These consist of a softwood outer frame with an infill of thin slats. They are available in heights from 1.2 m (4 ft) up to about 2 m (6 ft 6 in) and come in three basic designs: horizontal lap, vertical lap and interwoven. They are erected between wooden or concrete posts, and vary a great deal in quality and strength. Each panel should rest on top of a concrete or wooden (preferably hardwood) gravel board to prevent the panel from rotting. Trellis topping and/or defensive planting will be required to deter climbing. When constructing this type of fence with wooden posts, it is important to use galvanised metal brackets to fix the panels

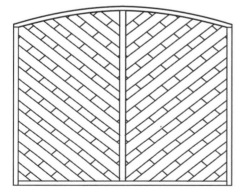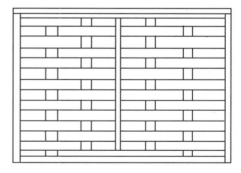

Two types of interwoven panels

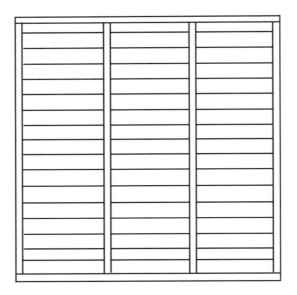

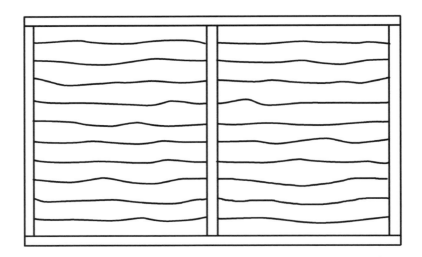

Two types of horizontal lap panels

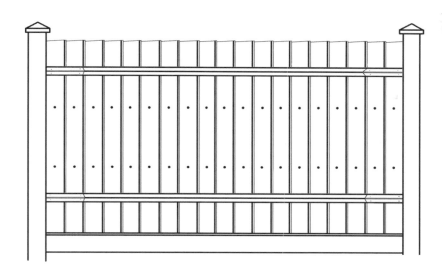

Vertical close-boarded panel

to the posts so that they cannot be lifted out or blown out by strong winds. If you are using concrete posts, secure each panel to its neighbour using a suitable metal strap, otherwise the panels could be lifted up and out of the slots in the posts.

HORIZONTAL-BOARD OR RANCH

This type of fence comprises posts and horizontal boards (rails). It is often quite low and generally used as a simple boundary marker to the front of a property. Because there are gaps between the boards, a high fence of this type can be scaled just like a ladder, so it is not suitable for security purposes.

VERTICAL CLOSE-BOARDED

This is a very common fence and one that is easy to construct. It comprises wooden posts set no farther apart than 3 m (10 ft)

with horizontal arris rails fixed between the posts. Vertical boards (often tapered in profile and known as feather-edge) are nailed to the rails. Two rails are used for a fence that is lower than about 1 m (3 ft), and three for higher fences. A 2-m (6 ft 6-in) fence built in this way, with the posts no more than 2.4 m (8 ft) apart, will provide a reasonable level of security, provided it is topped with trellis. The arris rails should be on the 'private' side of the fence, otherwise they can be used for climbing. If the fence marks a boundary with public land, reduce the distance between the posts to 1.8 m (6 ft). This also makes sense if the fence is exposed to strong winds. To prevent the vertical boards from rotting, include wooden (preferably hardwood) or concrete gravel boards at the base of the fence. Make sure that the gravel boards are well secured

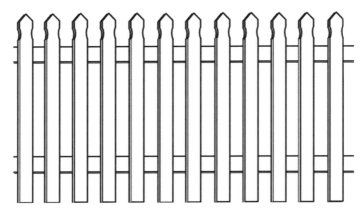

Wooden palisade

and the ground beneath them levelled. Otherwise, it might be possible to kick them out, allowing a burglar to crawl underneath.

You can increase the strength of a boarded fence by weaving steel straps between the boards as you nail them in place. You can also top the fence with trellis and prickly climbers, or cut the top of each board at a 45-degree angle to create a saw-tooth effect.

PALISADE AND STOCKADE

This is similar to the vertical close-boarded fence, but the boards are thicker and have gaps between them. This type of fence is often used where a back garden borders a canal or pathway, allowing the route to and from the garden to be observed. Passers-by will also be able to see into the garden, discouraging the would-be intruder, although many home owners may prefer the privacy provided by a solid fence. Because the boards of this type of fence do not overlap or fit tightly together, it may be easier for a

burglar to pull them off. To make this more difficult, they should be secured to the arris rails with coach bolts and washers, with the nuts on the inside of the fence. A fence bordering such a public area (which could be deserted at night) should stand 2 m (6 ft 6 in) high and have three arris rails. It can be topped with trellis, or you can cut the tops of the boards to form points. Defensive prickly plants can be allowed to climb up this type of fence, and you can grow thorny shrubs around the bottom. This will help solve any privacy concerns.

PICKET

A picket fence is similar to a palisade fence, but it is no more than 1.4 m (4 ft 7 in) high. You can deter anyone from sitting on such a fence by giving each upright a pointed top. Picket fencing that is less than 1 m (3 ft) high is often used as a simple boundary marker around an open-plan front lawn to keep animals and people off the grass. A picket fence that is about 1.2 m (4 ft) high combined with

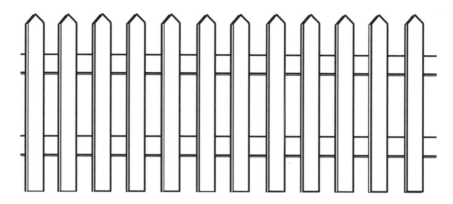

Picket fence

thorny hedging can create quite a useful barrier. Check with the planning authority if you intend putting a small fence around an open-plan front lawn, as there may be a condition in the original planning permission for the house that prevents you from doing so.

WATTLE PANEL

Wattle fence panels consist of a frame of stout upright branches interwoven with horizontal thinner branches. They are available in a variety of heights, but normally are around 1.8 m (6 ft) in width. As a rule, they are used as decorative

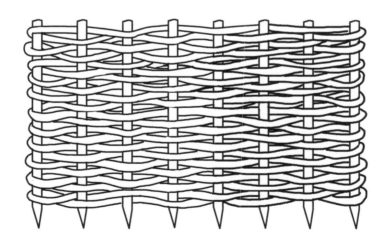

Wattle panel

19

fencing, although if suitably anchored between sturdy posts, they can be difficult to climb. This rather temporary fence is not suitable if you want security.

CHESTNUT PALING
This is another temporary fence, which you will often see in public parks and gardens protecting areas of reseeded ground. It consists of chestnut stakes wired together and is about 1-1.2 m (3-4 ft) high. It's useful for protecting a newly planted hedge and can be left in place while it matures.

Trellis toppings
Topping a wooden fence with trellis can stop a burglar from climbing over. The strength of trellis used in this way lies in its weakness. This may sound daft, but

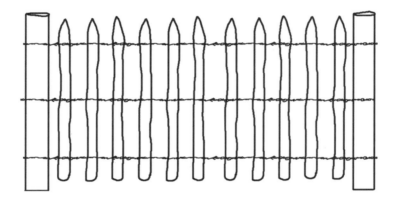

Chestnut paling

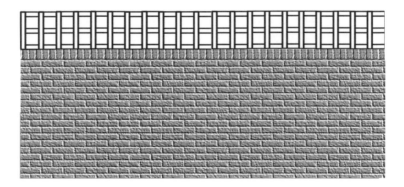

Brick wall topped with trellis

that is precisely the way it works. A burglar knows that it may collapse if he attempts to climb over (risking injury), so he's faced with the choice of trying to pull it down (difficult if it carries a thorny rose) or moving on to an alternative target. Most lightweight trellis will not take the weight of a person climbing over it. However, the heavyweight type, made from battens around 20 mm (¾ in) thick can be climbed, particularly if the trellis has been fixed to wooden fence posts or slotted into concrete posts. If you use the thicker type of trellis, you'll have to fix it well enough so that it doesn't fall down under the weight of a climbing plant, but will collapse if anyone steps on it.

Trellis can also be used to top brick walls. First screw vertical battens to the inner face of the wall, spacing them to match the width of the trellis panels. Then fix the panels to the battens with galvanised nails or corrosion-resistant screws.

Other toppings

If you want to improve your security in a more natural way, you could try training a thorny plant on wires along the top of the fence or wall. You'll need to increase the height of the fence posts by about 300–400 mm (12–16 in), which can be done by screwing wooden battens or lengths of angle iron to the posts or wall. Then the wires can be stretched between them.

For a domestic setting, it is not recommended to use 'aggressive' toppings, such as broken glass, razor tape and barbed wire. These are designed to cause injury and have been known to harm innocent persons, which can lead to the householder being sued. In fact, some aggressive fence toppings are not too difficult to overcome. For example, barbed wire can be cut with a decent pair of wire cutters, while broken glass can be climbed over by laying a heavy coat over it. The horticultural approach – using trellis and thorny plants – can be just as effective and, equally important, can be far more aesthetically pleasing.

If you do employ injurious toppings on a fence or wall, such as barbed wire or razor tape, the Occupiers Liability Act requires you to provide prominent warning signs on or near the barrier to indicate the risk of injury if anyone attempts to climb it. Never use such toppings on a fence that is less than 2 m (6 ft 6 in) high, and never hide anything unpleasant, such as carpet gripper, on the inside of a fence, as you could end up in court if someone is injured by it, even if he is a burglar. Under the Highways Act, if the fence borders a public highway, the council can order you to remove the topping if they consider it dangerous.

Divisional fencing

If a burglar can climb into a nearby garden from the street or an alleyway, it might be possible for him to scale a few of the divisional fences between neighbouring gardens and reach yours. You'll obviously have to make your own judgement about this, since if your house is, say, five or six gardens along from the house where the initial access could be gained, you're probably not at that much risk. To make it more difficult for a burglar to get into your garden from a neighbour's, you can top the fence with trellis or grow thorny shrubs along the length of the fence. If you like to chat to

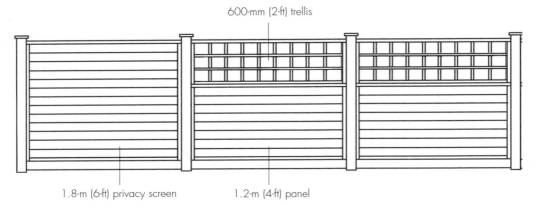

600-mm (2-ft) trellis

1.8-m (6-ft) privacy screen   1.2-m (4-ft) panel

Trellis and panel fence

your neighbours over the fence, you can install a trellis-and-panel fence. This will not only increase your security, but also allow more light into the garden to the benefit of your plants.

A TRELLIS-AND-PANEL FENCE

Start at the house end of the garden with a 1.8-m (6-ft) high fencing panel, which will act as a privacy screen. Then continue the fence with 1.2-m (4-ft) panels topped with 600 mm (2 ft) sections of lightweight trellis to give a total height of 1.8 m (6 ft). This creates a 'gossip fence'. If you don't like the idea of looking at your neighbour's washing line, you can gain more privacy by growing thorny shrubs through the trellis. The combination of the trellis and the shrubs gives you two layers of security – either the thorns will get the burglar or the fence will collapse with him on it, or preferably both! This type of fence is ideal for long, narrow gardens where a more traditional 1.8-m (6-ft) fence would be a little overbearing.

Types of metal fence

CHAIN-LINK FENCING

This type of fencing material is commonly found around schools and sports facilities, although it is often found in domestic gardens, particularly where the householder wants to maximise the amount of light falling on the garden. The plain galvanised or plastic coated, interwoven steel mesh is supplied in rolls by fencing companies and some building materials suppliers. It is attached by clips or tie wires to straining wires, which are stretched between concrete or metal posts set in concrete. Straining stays fitted to the posts are used to tighten the straining wires. For a firm fence that will last for years, the straining wires should be as tight as possible. Two wires are required for a fence up to 1.2 m (4 ft) high, and three wires for a fence up to 2.25 m (7 ft 4 in) high. If you dig a trench beforehand, you can bury the bottom 150 mm (6 in) of the mesh into the ground to prevent animals from getting under it.

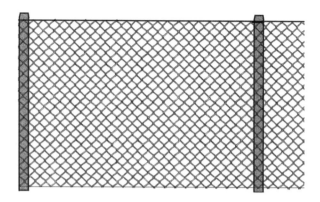

Chain-link fence

Ordinary chain-link fencing provides limited security, as it is easy to climb – the gaps in the mesh provide perfect finger- and toeholds. The wire is also easy to cut, enabling an intruder to unravel the mesh and climb through. Chain-link fencing can be made more secure, however, if used as a frame for a climbing thorny plant; in some instances, this can create an almost impenetrable barrier. The hedging plants should be planted on each side of the fence, so you'll need to set it back a little to plant the shrubs on your own land.

Although not designed for domestic use, the more robust, Class 2 anti-intruder chain-link fence can be installed in high-risk areas. This stronger fence uses a heavier mesh and straining wires, which are more difficult to cut, while the bottom of the mesh can be buried in a gravel trench to prevent anyone from crawling underneath.

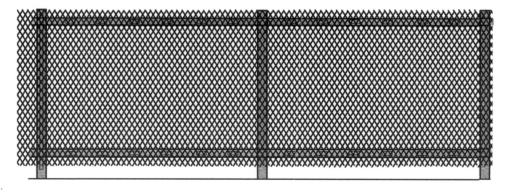

Expanded-mesh fence

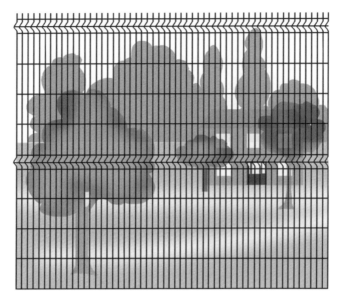

Welded-mesh fence

EXPANDED-MESH FENCING

Expanded-mesh fencing panels are punched from single sheets of steel and stretched to the desired panel size. Panels are galvanised and powder coated in a wide variety of colours. This type of fencing is stronger and more difficult to cut than standard welded-mesh panels or chain-link fencing, and is difficult to climb. Attempts to cut it can result in very sharp edges. A fencing system using this material would come with its own metal fence posts, although the panels can be attached to wooden posts if necessary.

WELDED-MESH FENCING

Although traditionally this product has been used in commercial and industrial settings, welded-mesh fencing has become very popular as an alternative to wooden fencing. The material is particularly useful where a view beyond the boundary of the property is desired. Welded-mesh panels are available in a wide variety of colours and designs. They consist of vertical and horizontal wires that are welded together where they cross. This makes them more secure than the standard chain-link fence. As with expanded-mesh panels, a welded-mesh fence would normally be erected using its own steel framework, but it is possible to fix the panels to wooden posts. The meshes come in a variety of sizes, the smallest being best suited to deter climbing, as it is difficult to gain finger- or toeholds. When viewed head-on, welded-mesh panels tend almost to vanish against their background, depending on their colour. Used with defensive plants, welded-mesh can create

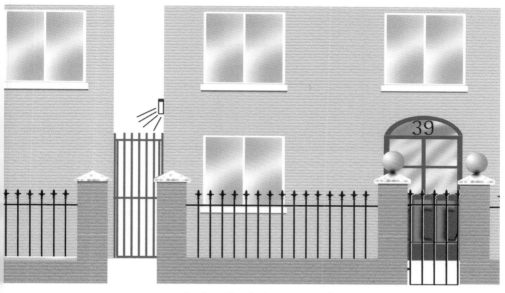

Brick wall with decorative railings

a strong and secure fence, although if you want to see through the fence, you'll have to choose the plants carefully for their height and spread.

RAILINGS

Cast-iron railings were widely used by the Victorians, but sometimes their decorative aspect far outweighed their usefulness as a security barrier – many incorporated myriad foot- and handholds. That being said, there are some fine surviving examples of Victorian railings that were deliberately designed to deter intruders with 'spearheads' and razor-sharp spikes.

Finial

More recently, the popularity of railings has returned, with attractive examples being used in a variety of new housing developments to create private space. They are useful as a boundary marker and intruder barrier, particularly when combined with a matching gate. An added bonus is that they permit anyone approaching the house to be seen easily from both inside and beyond the property.

Although cast-iron railings are still widely available, many modern railing systems are constructed from box-section or tubular steel, topped with a variety of decorative features, including ornamental spheres and pointed finials. When choosing the topping for railings, select something that will be difficult to climb over, but not potentially injurious. If you

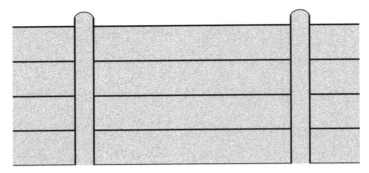

Concrete fence

intend putting railings on a low wall that borders a busy street, position them as near to the front of the wall as you can to prevent anyone from sitting on it.

Types of wall

CONCRETE-SECTION

A concrete-section wall consists of a number of concrete slabs slotted one on top of another between concrete posts. It provides a substantial barrier and plenty of privacy, and is cheaper to construct than a brick wall. Concrete walls require little or no maintenance, but they're not very attractive and are rarely used in modern housing developments. They also attract graffiti, which can only be tackled by applying an anti-graffiti glaze before any vandalism can be carried out.

CONCRETE SCREEN

Made from pre-cast concrete blocks with moulded open patterns, screen walls are popular alternatives to solid structures. The blocks are stack bonded – set one on top of another so that the vertical mortar joints run continuously from the bottom of the wall to the top. They must be supported at each end by concrete pillar supports (pilasters) or brick piers. If the span of the wall is more than 3 m (10 ft), intermediate supports will be required.

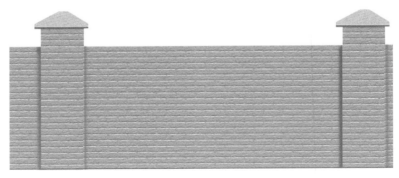

Brick wall supported by brick pillars

The disadvantage of this type of wall is that it provides a ready-made climbing frame for a burglar. However, defensive shrubs can be trained to grow against it. A screen wall allows the ground beyond the property to be observed easily.

BRICK

A 2-m (6 ft 6-in) brick wall capped with steep-sided coping stones will provide a reasonably secure boundary, but will be expensive to construct. Such a wall will require a substantial concrete foundation, but will need little maintenance for many years. To prevent rainwater from penetrating the top of the wall, the coping stones are normally bedded on a damp-proof membrane. The maximum safe height of a freestanding 100-mm (4-in) thick brick wall without piers is only 300 mm (1 ft). Walls above this height need to be built with supporting piers at intervals of 1.8–2.4 m (6–8 ft).

To stop people from sitting on a front garden wall, build it to the maximum height of 1 m (3 ft) and top it with steep-sided coping stones or railings. Alternatively, grow a thorny plant against the wall in the front garden.

Brick wall capped with steep-sided coping stones

Hedges

For hundreds of years, hedges of hawthorn, beech and other impenetrable thorny species have been used in the countryside to define and separate parcels of land, and contain livestock. In suburban gardens, hedges are grown primarily to define ownership, but also are an attractive security alternative to the fence, while providing additional privacy and a means of screening unsightly views, such as dustbins and sheds.

It is not uncommon for hedges in a back garden to be grown to a height of over 2 m (6 ft 6 in). The higher the hedge, the greater protection it will provide, but bear in mind that it will also create more shade, and draw more water and nutrients from the soil. The ideal height for a front-garden hedge is around 1.2 m (4 ft). This will allow your neighbours and passers-by to see any suspicious activity in front of your house, and permit you to monitor any activity around your neighbours' homes from your windows.

Refer to the plant list at the back of the book (*see Chap 10*) for shrubs that are suitable for hedging, and check the soil and growing conditions required before making your purchase. Do remember that prickly hedges cannot distinguish between friend and foe, and may fight back! Some varieties of hedging plant will grow quickly and require regular pruning.

A new hedge can take up to five or six years to establish itself as an effective barrier against intruders, but the reward is a natural boundary 'wall' full of berries and flowers, and foliage that changes colour with the seasons. If you want to plant a hedge, make sure that there is enough room for it in your garden, so that

it does not spill into a neighbour's property. If the hedge is to be planted on the boundary, talk to your neighbour first, as they may have a vested interest in sharing the cost. Remember, however, that a hedge is like a fence – if it's too high, it may hide the burglar.

Flats

Very often, there won't be a physical barrier surrounding a block of flats, just an open grassy space. This can be abused by those who regard land without a barrier as land without an owner. Poor design of the buildings and the grounds, and a lack of maintenance can quickly encourage anti-social behaviour. It is easy to highlight practical design problems, and some of them are easily remedied by using the principles of defensible space. One of the best ways to tackle these sorts of problem is to form a residents' association or neighbourhood watch and approach the landlord as a group. This can be very effective. For example, the residents of one estate in Birmingham became actively involved in a major refurbishment programme during the 1990s and saw their crime rate fall by 50 per cent within six months of completing the work; it has continued to fall ever since. Individually you can do a lot to improve your flat's security, but that's not always enough; sometimes, you need the landlord to work with you and your neighbours to develop wider-reaching improvements (*see Chaps 2 & 3*).

BALCONIES

Until quite recently, balconies were not considered to be particularly vulnerable unless they were on the ground floor. However, there has been an increase in the number of burglaries carried out where a balcony was the means of entry or was used as a climbing frame to reach other balconies above the ground and first floors. In addition, there has been a change in the way we use balconies.

These days, balconies are often used as storage spaces for expensive property, such as bicycles. The owner of a costly mountain bike, who is not happy about leaving it outside locked in a cycle rack, may carry it up several flights of stairs and leave it on their balcony in the belief that it will be safer, only to discover later that some athletic thief has scaled the balcony and dropped the bike down to his mate during the night. So if you have no option but to keep a bike on a balcony, make sure you secure it to a wall bracket, railing or balcony support using a 'D' lock or padlock and chain (*see Chap 5*).

Many balconies have attractive displays of hanging baskets, window boxes and planted tubs, which can be expensive to replace if stolen. Consequently, they should be secured (*see Chap 5*). You can deter a burglar by training a thorny plant through the railings of a balcony, either from the ground if it is on the ground floor, or from a large container, but make sure that the plant is tied firmly to the railings or support structure.

A balcony's security has a direct effect on the security of your home. If it is above first-floor level, it is probably less at risk, but ask yourself the following questions:

- How easy would it be to gain access to the balcony?

- Are the balconies of my block arranged one on top of another?

- Is there an alternative means of escape?

- If I were on the balcony, would I be noticed?

- If I were seen and noticed, would anyone react?

If access can be gained to the balcony, you will have to secure the doors and windows that open on to it as if they were on the ground floor (*see Chaps 3 & 4*).

A water boundary

Throughout history, water has been used successfully as a means of security. On many occasions, defensive water filled ditches around castles and towns have proved their worth by keeping unwanted visitors at bay. While we're not suggesting that you hire a mechanical digger to create a moat around your home, you may be lucky enough to live next to a deep stream, river or canal, which will provide a little extra security. The average opportunist thief will think twice before wading through murky water to burgle a house, especially if that is his only means of escape. Obviously, the depth of the water and its rate of flow will determine its true value as a barrier, but sometimes the psychological effect of a stretch of water can be very effective – many would-be intruders simply can't be bothered to take their shoes off!

If the back of your home faces directly on to a river or canal – and there is no tow path or public access between – you may want to take full advantage of the view and not put up a high fence. This is a reasonable decision, as it is unlikely that a burglar would select a river as a means of entry, unless he approached the premises by boat. During the summer, rivers and canals tend to attract increased boat traffic, and vessels may be moored overnight near the boundary of your property. If you are concerned about overnight trespass on to your land from moored boats, erecting a low fence can be effective without obstructing the view.

Many new homes have been built beside canals and around canal basins, and with them have come new or widened footpaths. These can increase the risk of burglary, especially if a footpath is under-used. If a path runs past the back of your home, make sure that the fencing is adequate; if you prefer a low fence, make doubly sure that your home itself is secured. In such circumstances, it would be wise to install an intruder alarm, with the bell box clearly visible from the footpath.

A combination of ponds and deep streams, together with a selection of naturally defensive plants in your back garden, can create an effective barrier and a natural habitat for wildlife. Low-level fencing, hedging or ornamental railings can reduce the chance of accident without affecting the deterrent value of the water. As a general rule, the deeper and wider the water, the less accessible to the public your propery becomes.

As with all security measures, you must consider all eventualities. A summer drought can reduce a water barrier to an ineffective trickle, so it is sensible to regard a river or stream as a security bonus and ensure that you have taken enough other security steps to protect your home.

CHAPTER 2

Access opportunities

The majority of burglaries and thefts from domestic properties are opportunistic. The burglar may get out of bed in the morning and decide to commit a crime, but that doesn't mean that he will have a target in mind. He will go to a favoured area where he thinks he can steal items of value and walk or drive around the streets looking for an easy opportunity to get into a house or garden. His planning tends to be done on the spur of the moment: having found a likely target, he weighs up the chances of being seen and caught against the possible rewards. Easy access is often the trigger that tips the balance in favour of taking the risk.

The majority of domestic break-ins tend to take place at the side or rear of a house, or in blocks of flats with corridor access (as opposed to those with well overlooked balcony access). A burglar will normally only attempt to enter the front of a property if there is a feature that makes it easy for him. This could be a deeply recessed front door, an open ground-floor window, a lack of lighting or, perhaps, a high hedge that shields the property from the street. There are five main types of access opportunity for the burglar – this chapter will show you what to do about them.

1 Side access

A path or drive at the side of a detached or semi-detached property can be quite vulnerable. In some cases, this will have a gate that opens on to the back garden. In this situation, however, the burglar can often climb over or force the gate with little likelihood of being seen from the street or neighbouring house.

SOLUTION 1 ADD A NEW GATE

One solution to the problem is to place an additional gate or gates across the path or drive at the front of the house so that any attempt to climb or force a way in will be visible from the street. The new gate should be at least 1.8 m (6 ft) high and be designed to resist forcing and climbing. It should also allow the side of the house to be observed, just in case a determined individual manages to get in and attempts to break open a side window. A single gate should be locked into its frame using a BS3621, kite marked mortice sash lock, which will allow the gate to be unlocked from both sides. A double gate should be secured with a hasp, staple and padlock, the second opening gate also having a sturdy bolt that shoots into the ground. It is sensible to fit rubber stops to prevent the gates from slamming into adjacent walls, and to have some means of securing them in the open position so that vehicles and bulky items can pass through safely, especially on a windy day. If the gates open directly on to the street, they must open inwards. If possible, fit a light above the gate to deter anyone from attempting to climb over it after dark.

You will require planning permission for a gate that is over 2 m (6 ft 6 in) high, or if it is placed immediately next to the public footpath or street and is over 1 m (3 ft 3 in) high. It is always best to check with the local planning

Common access opportunity down the side of two houses

department to make sure you won't be contravening any rules. Obviously, if the pathway or drive is shared with a neighbour, you will need their agreement first because you will both have to take responsibility for closing and locking the gate.

Forward positioned metal gates preserving surveillance of the sides of both houses

SOLUTION 2 IMPROVE AN EXISTING GATE

If you can't reach agreement with a neighbour or put up a second gate for some other reason, you will have to make the best use of the existing side gate. Ideally, this should be at least 1.8 m (6 ft) high, and be designed to deter climbing and resist forcing. In this case, you need the gate to be solid to prevent an inquisitive intruder from seeing what there is to steal from your back garden or use to break into your home. A side gate can be locked in the same way as a front gate, but normally you need only use a hasp, staple and padlock, or a padbolt, which is secured with a padlock.

2 Access from open land and railway lines

Some properties are particularly vulnerable to burglary and garden theft because their gardens back on to open countryside or land that is accessible to the public. The latter includes public parks and gardens, railway lines and canal tow paths. Railway lines are a particular problem, as they often run through deep

Securing existing side gates with trellis topping

cuttings that can't be observed from nearby houses. As a rule, the closer your property lies to a railway access point, such as a level crossing or station, the more vulnerable it is to intrusion. From a security point of view, a canal tow path can be likened to a back alleyway, but while an alleyway can often be gated and secured, a canal tow path cannot.

IMPROVE YOUR FENCING

The only option you have is to improve the strength, height and climbing resistance of your back-garden fence. If you have experienced problems and want to improve the security of your boundary still further – by planting defensive shrubs on the land beyond the fence, for example

– you must gain permission from the landowner first. Local authorities have a legal responsibility to do all that they reasonably can to prevent crime. Thus, you could approach the council's parks department and ask them to consider a defensive planting programme for the vulnerable perimeters of a public park to prevent adjacent homes from being burgled.

3 Access around blocks of flats

It is not possible to consider every access problem associated with the grounds of blocks of flats, because they are all so very different in layout and specific features. Most anti-social behaviour that occurs

33

around a block of flats tends to result from a lack of effective access control into the grounds and its buildings, the absence of secure private gardens for the ground-floor flats, a proliferation of under-used footpaths and often simply poor design.

To get an idea of the potential problems and their solutions, consider the following real example of some blocks of flats in London.

On the south side of the site were three blocks of flats, each of four storeys, with six flats on each floor. A 4-m (13-ft) wide path separated each block. The blocks were set back from the road by 4 m (13 ft). Access to each block was through a centrally located, recessed entrance door approached by a set of steps from the footway. The boundary between the front gardens of the flats and the footway was marked by a privet hedge.

The site was bordered by a road and footway to the south, a public footpath to the north, and wooden fences to the east and west. An overgrown hedge ran alongside the public footpath within the plot. A communal back garden occupied an area that was twice the area of the flats.

The residents of these blocks experienced a variety of problems, including burglary of the ground-floor flats through their back windows, theft of potted plants from the communal garden, trespass, littering and damage to the garden by young people late at night. Things came to a head when the residents found that drug users had been preparing and taking drugs in the shelter of their street doorways. The police were regularly called to the flats to deal with the problems, and it became clear to the landlord that improvements had to be made.

THE SOLUTION

Working together, the residents, landlord and police crime prevention department came up with a number of measures to prevent or, at the very least, reduce the problems. The unrestricted access to the grounds had to be removed, which was achieved by erecting gates and railings across the paths that ran between the blocks. The entrance door problem was solved by moving the doors forward to eliminate the recess (*see also Chap 3*). The residents were keen to retain the large communal garden, so dividing it into plots was not supported. However, some lighting was installed in the garden to illuminate the areas directly outside the ground-floor windows, while the overgrown hedge running alongside the public footpath was removed so that the pedestrians who used it could get a clear view of the flats. The privet hedge to the front of the flats was trimmed to a height of 1 m (3 ft 3 in), the landlord promising that it would be maintained at this height. The measures introduced were affordable, but more importantly they made a difference to the residents' lives. In effect, they had turned the misused communal garden into a private space, and had increased the potential for observation by removing barriers to vision and increasing light.

If you are experiencing problems of anti-social behaviour around your block of flats, discuss your options with your landlord or managing agent and the local police crime prevention department. Most solutions will require some improvement to the boundaries, to prevent the wrong people from getting in, and to the lighting so that a determined intruder will be spotted more easily.

4 Access from an alleyway

Communal back alleyways can range from narrow, muddy paths to concreted roads for garage access. Before the spread of car ownership, most of the alleys associated with terraced housing were included in an estate to provide essential access to drains and for the residents to get to the backs of their houses to save them having to walk through their houses with garden rubbish. They were also used for refuse collections and essential deliveries. In some cases, where alleys have long been used as short-cuts, they have become established rights of way.

Although until recently nearly all the nation's alleys had open entrances, which allowed anyone to wander down them, many were actually built with gates, but over the years these have been removed, many during wartime in scrap-metal drives, and to allow access for firefighters and air-raid wardens during bombing. After the war, with reports of burglary being

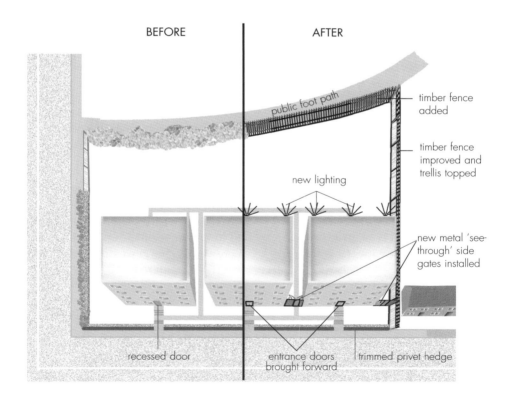

BEFORE   AFTER

public foot path

timber fence added

timber fence improved and trellis topped

new lighting

new metal 'see-through' side gates installed

recessed door

entrance doors brought forward

trimmed privet hedge

Securing the grounds around the blocks of flats (aerial view) much lower than they are today, it is understandable that only a small number of gates were put back.

Years later, the situation is very different, and as the number of burglary reports has increased so has the connection between the point of entry and the alleyway. The Home Office British Crime Survey shows that over 50 per cent of burglaries occur from the back of a property. That figure can grow to as high as 85 per cent if the house backs on to an alley. The alleyway can provide a burglar with a means of reaching his target unseen, and often a choice of escape routes without having to emerge into a road where he might be noticed. Some burglars carry out break-ins during the day when people are out and hide their ill-gotten gains in an alley, returning to collect them under cover of darkness. Of course, the alleyway itself can often be the scene of inappropriate behaviour.

Recently, a number of alley gating projects have been set up, with impressive results. In some instances where gates have been installed, rear-access burglaries have stopped altogether. It has even been shown that where some alleyways in an area have been gated, burglaries from all the surrounding alleyways have dropped as well, the burglars clearly having assumed that all have been protected.

The success of these initial alley gating projects led the Association of Chief Police Officers to publish the first alleyway gating guide, *The Alleygater's Guide to Gating Alleys*. A newer version, with the same title, was published by the Metropolitan Police in 2000 and can be downloaded from the Home Office Crime Reduction Website (*see Useful Contacts, p 49*).

The most successful alley gating scheme has been set up in Liverpool, where the crime prevention officer working with the Safer Merseyside Partnership (*see Useful Contacts, p 49*) has installed 4,000 gates, producing a reduction in burglaries in gated streets of up to 72 per cent.

GET HELP

If your house backs on to an alleyway and burglary is a problem, there are a number of issues to consider before embarking on an alleyway gating project. First, don't try to do anything on your own. Get together with your neighbours, and approach the local police and the council's community safety department. If you have a Neighbourhood Watch scheme operating in the area, get in touch with the organiser, as they are likely to have links to the local police and may already know about the problem alleys. As one of our crime prevention colleagues used to say about preventing crime, 'Whatever you do, don't get anxious, get advice!'

ARE THE ALLEYWAYS CAUSING THE PROBLEM?

This is an elementary question, but it is the key to the solution. You can find out more about crime in your neighbourhood by speaking with your local police and the community safety department of the local authority. They probably won't be able to give you specific addresses due to the confidential nature of the police reports, but they should be able to tell you the total number of burglaries in the streets around you and what percentage of them involved alleyways. This is vital information, particularly if your alleyway has a right of way over it; you will have to prove that it is clearly linked to the levels of crime before you can have the right of way removed.

Having obtained some official crime figures, it is worth speaking with anyone whose home backs on to the alley to obtain further information about anti-social behaviour in the area. Remember that a significant number of incidents are never reported to the police.

Plot the crimes you know of on an Ordnance Survey map, with a scale that is large enough to show individual houses. Take photographs of the alley entrances, and of any graffiti that you find or any other clue that could indicate anti-social activity. If the alleyway is maintained by the council and it attracts drug users, the council may have a record of the numbers of needles they have picked up along with other drug paraphernalia. You need to build a watertight case to prove to your neighbours, and possibly to the highways authority, that the problems in the alley are so bad that the only solution is to gate it.

INFORM YOUR NEIGHBOURS

Once you have obtained the crime information, and consulted the local police and council, you will need to meet with your neighbours. In the first instance, write to all of them who have a right of access along the alley, bearing in mind that a wider consultation will have to take place if it has an established right of way. Summarise your findings and the response from the police and local authority in the letter, and ask for your neighbours' views and support. If there is somewhere you can use for a public meeting, arrange a date and time, and invite them to attend. It's a good idea to add a tear-off response slip at the bottom of your letter for them to reply.

The response to your letter is likely to be positive from the vast majority of your neighbours. Even those who are not at first supportive (often because they are worried about the cost of the scheme) usually come around in the end. Be prepared to knock on the doors of those who do not respond to your letter. In most cases, it won't be because they don't support the idea; it is more likely that they're very busy people who have simply forgotten about it.

BE PATIENT

For a gating scheme to go ahead, you need the support of all those who may be affected, and protracted discussions may be necessary to achieve this. Quite rightly, everyone needs to be sure that what is planned is legal and that they will not suffer any detrimental side-effects. In some cases, you may need the services of a solicitor, or perhaps the advice of a senior fire officer about fire safety.

PLANNING PERMISSION AND PUBLIC RIGHTS OF WAY

Once you have obtained the support of your neighbours, you need to consult your local authority planning officer to determine if the gates require planning permission. If you do not live in one of the London boroughs, you also need to see the rights of way officer to establish if the alleyway has a public right of way running along it. In London, the planning officer can help with rights of way matters. A right of way can exist regardless of whether an alleyway is privately owned or adopted by a council.

Dear Neighbour

5th February

RE: GATING OUR ALLEYWAYS

You are probably aware of all the crime that's been taking place in our area and in particular in the alleyways. I have been speaking with the police and council about it and it seems that in the past 12 months our 120 houses have had 17 burglaries! The police told me that 14 of these were committed from the alley. Only two weeks ago my neighbour had her son's bicycle stolen from the back yard and just yesterday Mrs Baker found a used syringe outside her back gate! I'm sure you would agree with me that we have to do something about this and the police seem to think that by gating the entrances to our alleys we could really make a difference. They've shown me some gates already installed in some streets in Safetown, a mile away, and I was really impressed. I spoke to the lady who organised their gating project and she told me that since they were put up crime is much lower and everyone feels much safer.

I would very much like to know what you think about the idea and to start off I thought it would be right to drop you a line. I've organised a meeting at the Church Hall for 7pm on Thursday the 28th February and would love to see you there to get your views. In the meantime I would be most grateful if you could fill out the tear off slip and return it to me as soon as you can so that I've got some idea of how you think about it.

Regards,

Ivor Gate

Normally, planning permission will be required in the following circumstances:

- The gate is more than 2 m (6 ft 6 in) high – the most effective gates usually are.

- The gate will abut a highway – normally a footway or a road.

- The buildings are listed.

- The location for the gate is in a conservation area.

Therefore, in most cases, you will need planning permission. If the planning officer advises you that planning permission is required, try to deal with all of the gates in one application to save costs.

Until very recently, it would not have been possible to remove a right of way for the purposes of preventing crime. However, this situation was changed by the Countryside and Rights of Way Act 2000, which added a new section to the Highways Act (118B), permitting rights of way to be closed or diverted on the grounds of crime prevention. Of course, nothing is as simple as it may first seem, and for a local highways authority to obtain a closure order for an alleyway, they have to follow a set procedure.

First, the highways authority have to submit a report to the Secretary of State detailing the area in which they want to close or divert a right of way and giving all the reasons they wish to do so. If this is to prevent crime, they must show how the rights of way are contributing to the crime and specify the types of crime involved.

Once the Secretary of State has designated the area, the highways authority must seek an order from the Magistrates Court to close or divert the right of way. Once again, they have to make their case, this time specifying the right of way involved. At each stage of the process, the highways authority must invite objections from interested parties by posting notices at the entrances to the alley and placing adverts in local newspapers. In most cases, they will receive objections, and it is for the magistrates to consider these when making their decision about issuing an order. Until the courts have ruled on the matter, there can be no guarantee that you will be able to remove the right of way and gate the alleyway.

If you are faced with determined opposition, you may need to seek a compromise. Very often, a network of alleys will comprise a main 'through' alley which runs from street to street, with narrower paths branching off it to run behind the houses. In this situation, it might be possible to gate the branch paths and leave the 'through' route open, improving security by upgrading the walls and fences on each side of it.

Some organisations that are likely to oppose the gating of any alleyway will often state that there is no evidence to support police claims of reduced crime levels. However, there are many websites that provide a wealth of independent research giving clear evidence of the positive impact of gating. These can be found by searching the Internet for 'alleygates' or 'alley gates'. Make sure you print off and keep this information and use it to back up your case.

WHO OWNS THE ALLEY?

You must make all reasonable enquiries to establish ownership of the alleyway, as you will need permission from the owner to erect the gates. In many cases, however, it may not be possible to find out, as ownership would have remained with the original house builders, who may no longer exist. Sometimes, half each belongs to the owners of the houses that back on to it; in other cases, it belongs to the house owners along one side only, the others merely having rights of access. Examine your house deeds to establish what rights of access you have. If difficulties arise in respect of ownership, you should consult a solicitor in the first instance.

HOW MUCH WILL IT COST?

It is not possible to say exactly how much a gate will cost, but based on 2005 prices, expect to pay between £850 and £1,200 for a steel gate that satisfies the requirements given in this chapter. It is important to tell the manufacturer exactly what you want the gate to do by setting out the requirement. From this, the manufacturer will develop a suitable specification for you to examine.

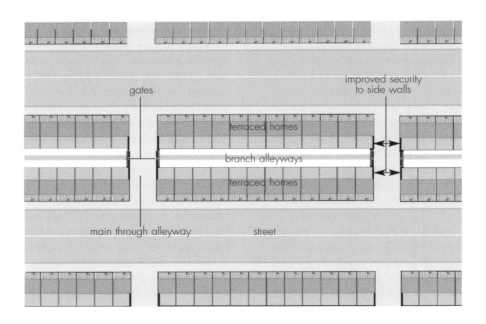

A compromise solution preserving access along the main through alleyway (aerial view)

You may be able to get a grant to help with your gating scheme, and the first step is to approach your local authority's community safety department. Some local authorities actively support gating projects and may be able to help in other ways. You could also seek the help of local businesses, which may benefit from an overall reduction of crime in the area.

There are, of course, other aspects to be costed. These include administration, such as letters, photocopying and stamps; maintenance – repainting, oiling and repairs, including clearing and cleaning the alleyway and its future maintenance; insuring the gates against claims of injury; and various legal fees for the planning application and, if necessary, removing a right of way. You may have to consider an annual charge on the residents, and many successful gating projects have led to the setting up of residents' associations not only to oversee the installation and maintenance of the gates, but also to act as a voice for all the residents on any issues that arise in future. Indeed, it is a good idea to set up a 'gating committee' or residents' association from the outset, with an elected chair, treasurer and so on. It should have its own bank account too.

Many alleyways become totally overgrown or filled with rubbish, all of which will need cleaning up before the gating scheme can go ahead. Some local authorities will provide a free community skip for this purpose, so it is worth asking.

SETTING OUT THE REQUIREMENTS FOR AN ALLEY GATE

Writing down the requirements for a gate will ensure that the maker of the gate knows exactly what you want it to do and where you want it installed. When the manufacturer has produced a suitable design, you can evaluate the gate against your needs; only when you are satisfied that all your requirements have been met should you part with the money. This is particularly important when you are handling a fund that has been donated by a large number of people. It is essential to keep your neighbours informed at every step of the way.

The table on pages 42–3 is a typical example of the requirements for an alley gate, which covers most needs. Use it as a basis for discussion with your neighbours before writing your own. The explanation and reasoning behind various points are given in italics.

You may not consider this an essential requirement, but it would be useful to install a low-energy light above the gate. Almost certainly, you will have to rely on one of the adjacent householders to do this, and although the gating funds can repay them for the cost of the installation, it is more than likely that they will have to accept the responsibility of maintaining the light, unless you can come to some financial arrangement to pay them for the electricity consumed and the cost of replacement bulbs.

DEALING WITH TUNNELS

In some cases, an alleyway starts as a tunnel that passes below an overhead building. In this situation, because climbing will not be a concern, you can have any design of gate you like. If there is a window directly above the gate, it would be wise to fit it with locks, even though a break-in through a front first-floor window is unlikely. The fire brigade

Typical requirements for an alley gate

For a 2.4-m (8-ft) high gate in a 1-m (3 ft 3-in) wide alleyway

1 The distance from the top of the gate to the surface of the alleyway will be no less than 2.4 m (8 ft).
Planning permission will be required if the gate is more than 2 m (6 ft 6 in high). Always check with the planning officer first.

2 The frame of the gate will be fixed into the end walls of both houses on each side of the alleyway.
If householders are concerned about the frame fixings causing damage to their house walls, it is possible to use freestanding frames set into concrete foundations. In some cases, an angled bar running back from the posts into an additional concrete foundation will be required for added strength. Check for drains, pipes and electricity cables.

3 The width of the gate and frame will match the width of the alleyway.
For wider alleys not used for vehicles, it may be necessary to use extension panels.

4 The gate will be constructed from steel and must be designed to deter people from climbing over it when it is closed and locked.
See illustrations for designs that make climbing difficult.

5 The gate will not be designed to deliberately cause injury to persons climbing over the top.
Gate toppings designed to cause injury should not be used. A 150-mm (6-in) blunted rod extension will make climbing uncomfortable for the casual intruder. Apart from the danger of causing injury to innocent people (children trying to retrieve a ball or police officers chasing a burglar), some of the more hostile toppings, such as spikes and razor tape, tend to exaggerate or confirm a high level of crime in the area, which drives up fear.

6 The gate will be installed in a position that is as near to the front walls of the houses as possible so that any attempt to climb it will be in view of the street, ensuring that the gate is sufficiently distant from any front garden walls that might provide a step-up.
Sometimes, garden walls can be about 1 m (3 ft 3 in) high, reducing the effective height of the gate to around 1 m. Setting the gate back by around 600 mm (2 ft) would be an acceptable compromise.

7 The gate will be designed so that public observation through the gate of both the alleyway and street is possible.
A solid gate that does not allow observation of the alleyway could actually help a burglar, especially if the adjacent house has ground-floor windows that face into the alleyway.

8 The gate and frame will be designed and installed to successfully resist opening by repeated kicking and bodily pressure, and must resist attempts at forcing, using easily obtained levers such as screwdrivers, chisels and crowbars.
See Useful Contacts, p 49.

9 The gate will be inward opening only and will not be self-closing.
The Highways Act makes it an offence to open any door, gate or bar over the highway unless you have express permission from the local highways authority. Provided the gate is well constructed, it does not matter if it opens inwards. Self-closing gates can be a nuisance when taking a bicycle or wheelbarrow through or when people are handling heavy loads.

10 The gap beneath the gate and frame will be no greater than 100 mm (4 in).
During the planning of gating schemes, some people have been worried about the

migration of wildlife along alleyways. Odd as this may seem to some, it is a genuine consideration, and steps should be taken to devise measures that at least allow the movement of smaller mammals, such as hedgehogs and mice. Don't dismiss this out of hand, as a gating scheme could be scuppered if you fail to deal with the concerns of all those involved.

11 It must not be possible for the gate to be lifted from its hinges in either the closed or open position.

12 All fixings of the gate and frame must be inaccessible when the gate is closed and locked.

13 The gate will be fitted with an automatic deadlocking mortice latch that is fit for the purpose of preventing forced entry, permitting the gate to be slammed and locked without the use of a key. The lock will be operated by key on both sides of the gate, and each gate will have a different key cylinder so that it is opened using a different key.
Although an automatic deadlocking latch is the best choice, with a different lock for each gate, there may be good reasons to alter this requirement. Ultimately, you must install a type of lock that will meet the needs of the majority of residents.

14 Two keys for each lock will be provided to each household for the one or two gates they nominate. Keys will be of the Master Locksmith Association recommended restricted type, and copies will only be provided on receipt of a letter of authority from the Residents' Association.
Each household may need more than two keys if it is normal practice to enter the house from the alley. Keys must be given to the residents on the day that the gates go up.

15 The lock and its fitting will not provide a foothold for climbing.
This can be achieved with a metal box gate by selecting a very narrow style of lock that will fit inside the box-section steel frame. An Adams Rite semaphore lock may be suitable (see Useful Contacts, p 49).

16 The gate, frame and house wall will include measures to dampen the noise of opening and closing.
A really important detail. Gates have been removed by the owners of houses to which they are attached because the clanging has driven them mad.

17 The gate, frame and fixings will be galvanised to resist rust.
Gates that are galvanised can be left in their natural finish or painted after they have weathered for a time. The manufacturer should be able to advise you on how long the weathering process should last. When painting the gate, you will have to apply a suitable primer before adding at least two undercoats and a top coat. Some manufacturers supply gates that are powder coated at the factory. This finish will last a long time, but you should still allow for repainting in your maintenance arrangements.

18 A light will be located above the gate (optional).
You may not consider this an essential requirement, but it would be useful to install a low-energy light above the gate. Almost certainly, you will have to rely on one of the adjacent householders to do this, and although the gating funds can repay them for the cost of the installation, it is more than likely that they will have to accept the responsibility of maintaining the light, unless you can come to some financial arrangement to pay them for the electricity consumed and the cost of replacement bulbs.

may insist that a gate in this situation is only bolted from the inside, rather than locked, to enable an easy escape from the alley in an emergency.

WHO WILL MAKE AND INSTALL THE GATE?

Locksmiths who are members of the Master Locksmiths Association can provide and install alley gates. They know about locks, think along security lines, normally are local to the area they serve and have a good knowledge of the potential crime risks. Some make gates themselves, while others may take the design to a steel fabricator. Alternatively, you may decide to approach one of the many specialist manufacturers that have sprung up in recent years. If so, start by going to the Police Secured by Design website and the gate manufacturers listed in the Useful Contacts. It is advisable to get three quotations.

NON-RESIDENT ACCESS

During the planning stage of your gating project, you must consider the non-residents who will need access to the

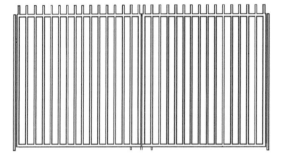

Typical gate arrangement for vehicle width alleyway

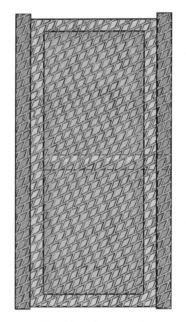

Metal box frame with expanded metal sheet

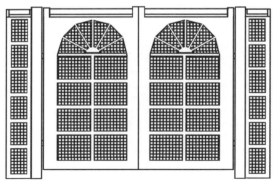

Perforated steel sheet gates and side panels with revolving top bar

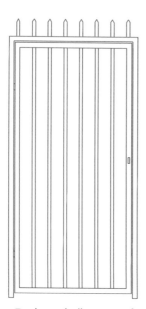

Traditional alley gate of
metal box construction

Rubber stop, the
purpose of which is
to reduce the noise
made by the gate
opening against
a wall

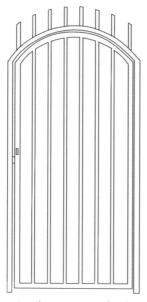

An alternative top finish

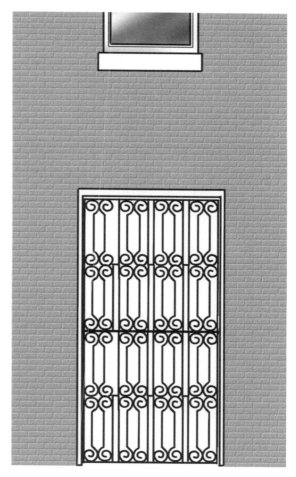

A tunnel gate

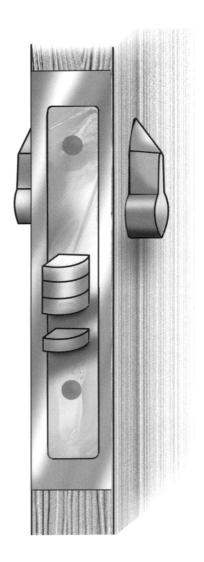

An example of an automatic
deadlocking mortice latch

alleyway. Depending on the type of alley, this can be quite a long list.

Fire Brigade Firefighters will always use the shortest route possible to reach the seat of a fire or someone who is trapped. This is unlikely to be an alleyway unless the building on fire is next to it. However, if the alleyway is wide and contains fire hydrants, you must ensure that the fire brigade have access to them. This may mean fitting a lock to the gate for which the brigade have keys. Normally, they are very positive about gating schemes and will do all they can to help. The important thing is to inform the local fire station commander about your plans and ensure that you follow his or her advice.

Utility companies Wide alleyways will often contain electricity cables, gas pipes, drains and sewers, and telephone and television cables and cabinets. In this situation, you must allow provision for their maintenance, and one way of doing this is to fit each gate with a sign giving contact details for several people locally who can open the gate. Bear in mind that the houses adjacent to the gate will be the ones whose doors are knocked on most regularly by non-residents wanting access, and their residents must be prepared to take on this responsibility.

Council refuse collection and maintenance Some alleys are still used as routes for refuse collection, the bins being left out by the back gates of the houses. Since gating, some councils have switched the bin collections to the fronts of the houses and have benefited from unexpected savings in time and costs for the operation. Additional savings have been made by not having to collect fly-tipped rubbish from alleys and destroy associated vermin. Fire brigades have reported big reductions in small rubbish fires, often set by children playing with matches. Moreover, a gated alleyway becomes a much safer place for children to play, because they cannot run out into the road and are less likely to encounter strangers.

In Liverpool, many gated alleyways are still maintained by the local authority. This forward thinking council was aware from the outset that residents living in the gated areas would not be able to bear the costs of maintenance and public lighting and have continued to accept this responsibility. However, they have made substantial savings in costs compared to when the alleys were open.

When the gates are installed, consider an official launch and invite the local police chief and councillor.

FINALLY...

Expect to take at least six months from the conception of the project to its completion. After the gates have been erected, you will need to meet with your committee on a regular basis to keep an eye on the gates and sort out any problems as they emerge. When they have been up for a year, reassess the crime information to see if things have improved. Let your neighbours know the results of the assessment.

There are huge advantages to be gained from gating a network of alleys that is blighted by anti-social behaviour. The good news is that, nowadays, most local planning authorities will not approve applications for new developments that include ungated pathways to the rear of houses and other buildings. It seems that the lessons of the past have been learned.

5 BASEMENT FLATS

A common feature of the large Victorian house is a basement, many of which have been converted into flats. Often, the front door of the ground floor is approached across a bridge over a light well that provides access to one or more basement flats. A single set of steps connects the street level with the light well and is gated at the top. Because the light-well steps are frequently used for emergency escape, the gate is left unlocked during the day or at all times when the building is occupied.

Burglars find these places attractive because they allow them to work unseen from the street. They also attract street based drug users, offering shelter and privacy.

ESSENTIAL ADVICE
Altering the access to a basement may conflict with a means of escape in an emergency. You should seek advice from the local authority's building control department before carrying out any work. You may also require planning permission.

LOCK THE GATE

The simplest method of preventing an intruder from gaining access to a basement light well is to lock the gate at the top. This will be reasonably effective if the railings and gate are of a climb-resistant design. In this instance, the railings should have a finial top or simple blunted-rod extension, a height of around 1.2 m (4 ft) and no footholds. If others share the same emergency steps, you won't be able to do this unless there is a fail-safe and easy method of unlocking the gate in an emergency. This arrangement

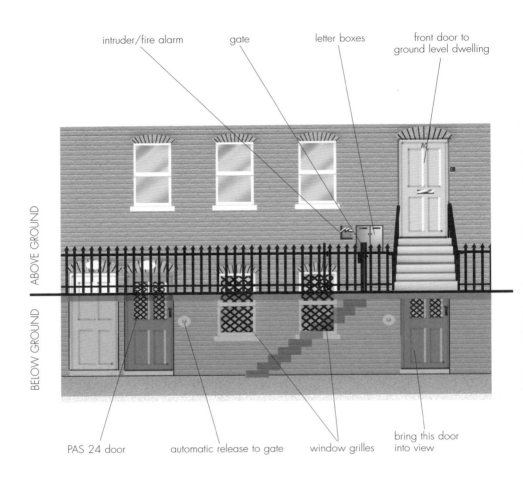

intruder/fire alarm gate letter boxes front door to ground level dwelling

ABOVE GROUND

BELOW GROUND

PAS 24 door automatic release to gate window grilles bring this door into view

Basement dwelling security issues

must satisfy the local authority. Even if no other households share the steps, you should still consider how you would unlock the gate in an emergency. Searching for a key in dense smoke is no joke. Locking the gate when you leave the premises unoccupied is not a problem, because the steps cease to be an emergency exit if there is nobody to use them.

At a basic level, you can provide a fail-safe means of unlocking the gate by protecting its (non-locking) bolt within a steel box that prevents operation from the street side. Unfortunately, this may then be used as a foothold, so it might be better if the gate could be unlocked automatically. This can be achieved with an electric deadlock or magnetic lock, both of which open when the electricity is cut. This could be arranged to occur with the activation of a fire alarm or manually by the operation of a switch at the bottom of the steps.

IMPROVE THE SECURITY OF THE DOORS AND WINDOWS

If you are unable to secure the gate at the top of the steps, your only option will be to increase the security of the doors and windows of the basement. Ideally, do this anyway. Because the basement is particularly vulnerable to burglary, your security improvements should be substantial. Window locks alone are not enough, and you should consider fitting internal or external security grilles, or internal concertina gates to the windows. The entrance door should be upgraded to a PAS 24 or fitted with an outer gate. If the door is hidden under the bridge to the ground-floor entrance, you could consider bringing it out into view, but you will need planning permission (*see Chap 3*). A high level of night-time lighting in the light well is essential.

USEFUL CONTACTS

Adams Rite Manufacturing Company
www.adamsrite.com

British Waterways
www.britishwaterways.co.uk

Decor-Grille Security
www.dgsecurity.co.uk

Expanded Metal Company
www.expandedmetalfencing.com

Home Office Crime Reduction Centre
www.crimereduction.gov.uk

Master Locksmiths Association
www.locksmiths.co.uk

Network Rail
www.networkrail.co.uk

Safer Merseyside Partnership
www.safermerseysidepartnership.co.uk

Secured By Design
www.securedbydesign.com/companies/index.asp

SWS UK
www.sws.co.uk

CHAPTER 3

Door security

The British Crime Surveys and police crime figures tell us that around 40 per cent of burglaries occur through doors. Remember, however, that this is a national picture of the risk. For example, if you live in a third-floor flat with a private entrance door off a corridor, and no windows on to the corridor, a burglar will always have to break in through the entrance door. If you live in a terraced house with no rear access and a front door that is deeply recessed, the chances are that a burglar will try to force the front door. Consequently, you need to carry out your own risk assessment to identify the weaknesses that are specific to your home.

SECURITY STANDARDS FOR DOORS
High risk
LPS1175 SR 6
LPS1175 SR 5
The attack tests carried out against products of these standards will employ a variety of powerful, mains operated tools for up to 30 minutes for each test.

Medium risk
LPS1175 SR 4
LPS1175 SR 3
The attack tests carried out against products of these standards will employ battery operated power tools for up to 30 minutes for Security Rating (SR) 4 and up to 20 minutes for SR 3 for each test.

Low risk
LPS1175 SR 2
BSI PAS24
LPS1175 SR 1
See main text for attack tests for these standards.

Doors come in a wide variety of types, made from a range of materials and locked in many different ways. It would be impossible to provide information on every type of door, but the information given in this chapter will deal with most. Don't forget that you can get further help and advice from the local police crime prevention department and by visiting local locksmiths.

High-security doors

Today, you can buy complete door sets (door, frame and locking mechanism) that have been manufactured to high levels of security. Two organisations in the UK have been involved in the creation of security standards for these door sets (and windows): the British Standards Institution (BSI) and the Loss Prevention Certification Board (LPCB). The following information deals mainly with the single BSI standard for domestic door sets because most of the sets available from the manufacturers to be found on the Police Secured by Design website have been tested to this standard. The LPCB have developed the LPS standard for door sets, which includes six security ratings depending on risk. Door sets manufactured to the Low Risk standards of BSI PAS24 and LPS1175 SR 2 are recommended for most domestic situations and are considerably more resistant to a burglar than the 'average' entrance door in most homes.

The attack tests carried out against products of these standards will employ a variety of hand tools – such as hacksaws, chisels, hammers and crowbars – for up to 15 minutes for SR 2 and BS PAS24, and up to ten minutes for SR 1 for each test. The BSI PAS24 standard is actually a higher standard than SR 1, but lower than SR 2.

The existence of these security standards is really important for anyone looking to replace their doors; visit the Secured by Design website for the very latest information on the standards and a large range of suppliers.

British Standards Institution PAS24-1 1999 is a test specification for improved security for a newly fabricated domestic door set, and covers both front and back doors. PAS stands for Product Assessment Specification, which is a forerunner to the well-known British Standard Kitemark. Door sets that have achieved PAS24 undergo a variety of test procedures, including lock manipulation, glazing security, mechanical loading, attack testing and tests that replicate shoulder charging and kicking. Ultimately, a PAS24 door set (including the door, doorframe and locking system) with at least 6.4-mm ($^1/_4$ in) laminated glass (if glazing is required) will afford a very good level of protection against forced entry.

It is important to note that PAS24 is a test of the whole door set, not the individual components, so beware of anybody who tells you that their doors use, for example, PAS24 locks or frame fixers. They might be excellent pieces of hardware, but they could be installed in sub-standard doors. Although it is possible to improve the security of an existing door using a range of high-quality locks and other security features, the improved door set could never be described as PAS24.

If you intend buying replacement doors (and windows) that meet the PAS24

ESSENTIAL ADVICE
If your door has a multi-point locking system, don't leave your home unoccupied without first engaging the locks. In most cases, this is done by lifting the outside handle, then deadlocking them by turning the key in the cylinder. Never leave the door closed on only the live bolt, even if you are just popping out for five minutes.

standard, make sure that the supplier provides you with evidence of the testing, such as a copy of the test certificate. You also need to obtain a manufacturer's signed declaration that all products supplied are identical to those tested.

If you have moved into a new home in the past five years that has gained the police Secured by Design award, the chances are that most of your external doors will comply with these standards.

Because locks are included in the PAS24 tests, you can be rest assured that they will comply with your insurer's requirements. However, although the Association of British Insurers (ABI) and its members, and other insurers who are not ABI members, recognise this standard, you must check with them first.

Doors conforming to PAS24 generally have a multi-point, deadlocking system with three or more deadbolts/hook bolts, or a combination thereof operated through a key cylinder. However, some have an automatic deadlocking rim lock fitted near the top of the door, and a mortice deadlock and boxed keep (Kitemarked to BS 3621:1998) near the bottom. The lock cylinders will meet the European Standard BS EN 1303 Grade 3.

SECURITY TIP
Sometimes, replacing a door can allow you to reposition it to remove a troublesome recess. Entrance doors should be sited so that callers at the door can be seen from neighbouring properties. Therefore, it is preferable to place them to the front of the property and not to recess them. If a door must be set back, the recess should not be more than 600 mm (2 ft) deep (*see 'Recessed door', pp 83–5*).

The front door

This is the street door that is normally used to enter and leave your home. It is also a means of escape in an emergency, something that must be borne in mind when considering locks. Most front doors can be secured in the same manner. However, differences do arise depending on the door's location. If your front door is above the ground floor, as in a block of flats, go straight to 'Private flat entrance door'. If your door is used by more than

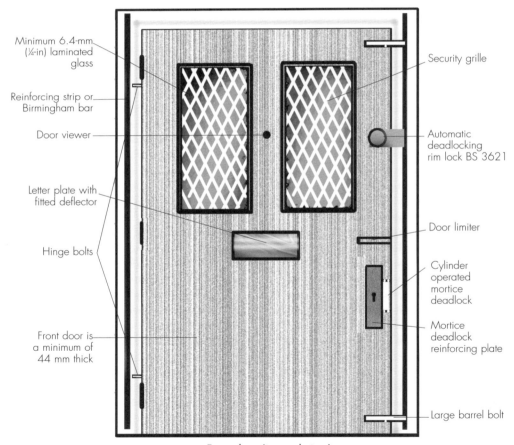

Minimum 6.4-mm (¼-in) laminated glass

Reinforcing strip or Birmingham bar

Door viewer

Letter plate with fitted deflector

Hinge bolts

Front door is a minimum of 44 mm thick

Security grille

Automatic deadlocking rim lock BS 3621

Door limiter

Cylinder operated mortice deadlock

Mortice deadlock reinforcing plate

Large barrel bolt

Front door (internal view)

one household, go straight to 'Communal entrance door'. The following information assumes that you intend to keep your existing door and not upgrade to a PAS24 door set. Information on security locks and hardware is given later in the chapter.

BASIC REQUIREMENTS

The front door Should have a solid core and be at least 44 mm (1³/4 in) thick.

The frame The frame should be secured to a brick wall with screws or frame fixers at maximum centres of 600 mm (2 ft) and 300 mm (1 ft) from each corner. If the wall is constructed from aerated concrete blocks, or if you think that the risk of burglary is particularly high, reduce this to 450-mm (1 ft 6-in) centres.

Hinges The door should hang on three hinges.

Hinge bolts Irrespective of the opening direction of the door, fit a pair of hinge bolts, 150 mm (6 in) below the top hinge and 150 mm above the bottom hinge.

Rim lock An automatic deadlocking rim lock (preferably to BS 3621) should be installed approximately a third of the door's height from the top.

Mortice deadlock A BS 3621 mortice deadlock with boxed keep should be fitted approximately a third of the door's height from the bottom, avoiding any joints in the frame.

Door limiter A door limiter should be fitted in the centre of the door.

Door viewer Fit a door viewer at a convenient height.

Letter plate deflector Fit this steel cowling over the letter plate on the inside of the door to prevent anyone from reaching the locks by hand or with a tool through the letter plate (*see p 78*).

ADDITIONAL SECURITY

Barrel bolts You can fit barrel bolts to the door for night use, but read the guidance notes carefully.

Security grille On a glazed door, prevent anyone from breaking the glass to reach the locks at night by fitting a security grille inside the glazed panel.

Laminated glass Ordinary glass should be replaced with 6.4- or 6.8-mm (¹/4 in) laminated glass, which will delay a glass breaking burglar (*see also 'Applied safety and security film', p 103*).

Reinforcing bars Fit a London bar to the inside of the frame on the locking side, and a Birmingham bar to the inside of the frame on the hinge side. See frame reinforcing bars later in this chapter.

Private flat entrance door

BASIC REQUIREMENTS

The door Your flat door should have a solid core and be at least 44 mm (1 ³/4 in) thick. It should provide a minimum of 30 minutes fire resistance and be self-closing.

The frame The frame should be secured to a brick wall with screws or frame fixers at maximum centres of 600 mm (2 ft) and 300 mm (1 ft) from each corner. If the wall is constructed from aerated concrete blocks, or if you think that the risk of burglary is particularly high, reduce this to 450-mm (1 ft 6-in) centres.

Hinges The door should hang on three hinges.

Hinge bolts Irrespective of the opening direction of the door, fit a pair of hinge bolts, 150 mm (6 in) below the top hinge, and 150 mm above the bottom hinge.

Rim lock A roller-bolt rim lock should be installed a third of the door's height from the top. This will prevent you from locking yourself out, as you have to lock it with a key from outside.

Mortice deadlock A BS 3621 mortice deadlock with boxed keep should be fitted a third of the door's height from the bottom, avoiding any frame joints.

It should have a cylinder key operation with a knob on the inside to allow emergency escape.

Door limiter A door limiter should be fitted in the centre of the door.

Door viewer Fit a door viewer at a convenient height (unless door glazing gives a view).

Letter plate deflector Fit this steel cowling over the letter plate to prevent anyone from attempting to reach the locks by hand or with a tool through the letter plate.

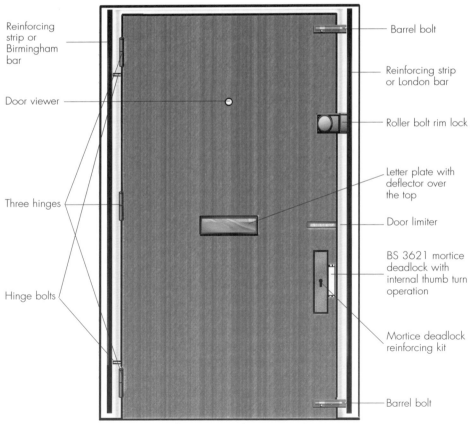

Private flat entrance door (internal view)

ADDITIONAL SECURITY

Barrel bolts You can fit barrel bolts to the door for night use, but read the guidance notes carefully.

Security grille On a glazed door, prevent anyone from breaking the glass to reach the locks at night by fitting a security grille inside the glazed panel.

Laminated glass Ordinary glass should be replaced with 6.4- or 6.8-mm laminated glass, which will delay a glass breaking burglar (*see 'Applied security film', p103*).

Reinforcing bars Fit a London bar to the inside of the frame on the locking side, and a Birmingham bar to the inside of the frame on the hinge side.

Extra door locks If your flat door is off a corridor and, therefore, not easily observed, you can increase its security by relocating the roller-bolt rim lock to the centre of the door and fitting a pair of BS 3621 mortice deadlocks (with internal knobs) about a quarter of the door's height from the top and bottom. You may require a new door.

Communal entrance door

The number of households using a communal entrance door can range from two to over a hundred, and the greater the number of users, the less secure it is likely to be. The police recommend that the maximum number of flats served by each communal door in a newly built block of flats should be between eight and ten, depending on the area and local risks. Above that figure, the sense of ownership of the door becomes diluted and the ability to recognise neighbours more difficult, allowing strangers to follow legitimate residents through the door without being challenged.

The communal entrance doors of blocks of flats often open outwards. This will always be the case if the door is a designated escape route and is likely to be used by more than 60 people in an emergency. Sometimes, this leads to the door being recessed so that it does not open over the public footway. Unfortunately, this can result in the recess being misused (*see 'Recessed door' p 83–5*).

The main advantage of an outward opening door is that it is more difficult to kick in against the doorstop. The main disadvantage is that it must be possible to open the door from the inside without a key during an emergency, such as a fire. Therefore, it is essential to ensure that the security hardware on such a door satisfies the apparent conflicting needs of fire safety and security.

In nearly every case, the landlord or the managing agent will carry out any work to the communal door and should employ personnel with the skills to do so. The list of police recommended security features for communal entrance doors given here can be given to your landlord and applied where appropriate.

If the door is to be replaced, it is sensible to fit a door approved to the relevant parts of BSI PAS24 or LPS1175 SR2/3 Grade 2 or higher. Encourage the landlord or managing agent to visit the Secured by Design website for manufacturers of communal entrance doors. If the security of an existing wooden door needs improving, ask the landlord or managing agent to consider the security features listed here. Existing steel, steel and timber, and other composite, UPVC or aluminium doors will not necessarily require all of these security measures.

The door and frame Communal entrance doors and door frames are subjected to a lot more wear and tear than a normal front door and must be constructed accordingly. Where applicable, door frames should be installed to the manufacturer's instructions. In general, a wooden frame should be fixed to the structure of the building (brick or block) using frame fixers at maximum centres of 600 mm (2 ft) – or 450 mm (1 ft 6 in) for fixings into aerated concrete blocks, or where the risk of intrusion is particularly high – and 300 mm (1 ft) from each corner. The doorstops, if not integral rebates on a moulded frame, should be nailed and glued. Wooden doors should have a solid core and be at least 50 mm (2 in) thick.

Communal entrance doors are liable to damage from kicking or being held back against the door closer. A kick-plate will help prevent some of this damage. Panelled doors with rails and stiles can have a steel kick-plate fitted to the bottom rail, which should be around 400 mm

(1 ft 4 in) high. The top rail of a panelled door should be of sufficient size to accommodate a door closer.

To increase the strength of the door, a metal T-bar can be fitted along the length of its opening edge. This will extend the edge of the door to cover the gap between the door and frame, preventing any sort of lever, such as a crowbar, from being inserted. It will also prevent access to the live bolt of a mechanical lock (*see below*).

The plywood inserts of some panelled doors are very thin and easily kicked in, the most vulnerable being those at the bottom of a door or the bottom of any side panels. Additional strength can be provided by replacing thin panels with thicker external-grade or marine plywood. The thickness of the replacements will be determined by the depth of the rebates, but ideally they should be at least 12 mm ($^1/_2$ in) thick. In some cases, the new panels will have to be placed over the existing ones, overlapping the rails and stiles. They should be screwed and glued in place.

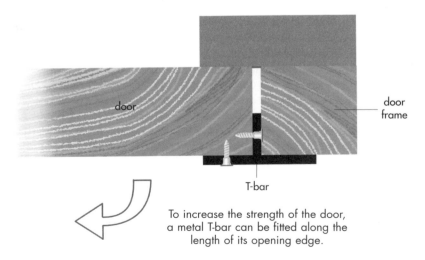

door

door frame

T-bar

To increase the strength of the door, a metal T-bar can be fitted along the length of its opening edge.

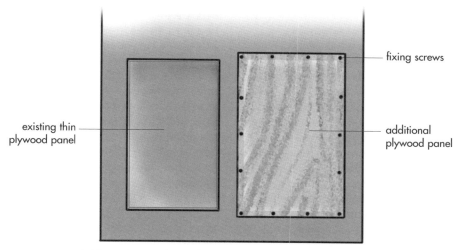

existing thin
plywood panel

fixing screws

additional
plywood panel

Additional strength can be provided by replacing thin panels
with thicker external-grade or marine plywood.

Communal entrance doors should not be recessed; if possible, a door should be brought forward so that it is in full view of the street. If a recess cannot be avoided, it should be no deeper than the opening arc of the door and, ideally, no deeper than 600 mm (2 ft).

Glazing A burglar can easily break through ordinary glass to reach the inner handle of a door lock (required for emergency escape). Laminated glass (two sheets of glass sandwiching a layer of plastic) is a lot stronger than ordinary float glass or toughened glass and will delay an intruder, during which time he is vulnerable to discovery. Although more expensive than other types of glass, if it is broken or a burglar decides to give up, it can be replaced easily. Depending on the amount of damage, it may be possible to leave it in place, rather than installing temporary boarding. Toughened glass is made for safety purposes and breaks into tiny fragments to reduce injury. It must be specially made and can leave you with an unsightly boarded-up door panel for weeks.

Any glass used in the door or panels next to the door should be laminated and have a minimum thickness of 6.4 mm, but preferably 6.8 mm. The glass should be securely fixed into the frames in accordance with the guidelines set down by the Glass and Glazing Federation (*see Useful Contacts, p 85*). Alternatively, a small-gauge security grille can be fitted over the inside of the glazed panels.

Low-level glass panels are vulnerable to accidental and intentional damage, and provide an easy access opportunity for the burglar. They should be replaced or their security improved. You can replace the glass with external-grade plywood, using the thickest that will fit in the rebate, or simply install a 12-mm (^{1}/$_2$-in) plywood panel over the rails and stiles of the door. In either case, the plywood should be glued and screwed in place, and painted to match the door and side panels. To prevent the loss of natural light in the hallway, a third option is to fit a small-gauge security grille to the inside of the glazed panel.

Wherever possible, you should be able to see a caller at the door before opening it; you should also be able to see into a communal hallway before entering. For this reason, at least some glazing in the door is advisable. Moreover, loitering is far more likely in an entrance hall that cannot be observed from outside.

If there is no glazing in the door (common in houses converted to flats) or the glass is obscured (frosted), a door viewer must be fitted at a maximum height of 1.5 m (5 ft). An additional door viewer will be required for a wheelchair user or a child, although children should not answer the door to strangers. Alternatively, the door can be glazed with clear glass and protected as already described.

Hinges The hinges of outward opening doors are exposed, and burglars have been known to cut the tops off the hinge pins and remove them. In some cases, the hinge pin can simply be knocked through with a centre punch. Although this is unlikely to happen to a door at the front of a building, the method of protection is so cheap that it might as well be done anyway. Fit a hinge bolt 150 mm (6 in) below the top hinge and another 150 mm above the bottom hinge. Alternatively, have the doors rehung with locking hinges. Inward opening doors can also be fitted with hinge bolts or locking hinges to provide greater resistance to forced entry on the hinge side of the door.

Letter plates To make it difficult for a burglar to push a hand or tool through a letter plate to reach the lock handle, the letter plate must be located at least 400 mm (1 ft 4 in) from the lock. Further protection can be provided by fitting a letter plate deflector to the inside of the letter plate. This can also prevent the theft of car and house keys left on a hallway table. If the door is inward opening, it may be necessary to install some form of doorstop to prevent the deflector from hitting the wall.

Access control Controlling access to a block of flats at street level is an essential security requirement. If the communal door isn't locked, or there isn't a door at all, a burglar will be able to reach your private flat entrance door, and if that door opens on to an internal corridor, he will be able to force it without being seen from the street.

If you live in a top-floor flat, don't make the mistake of thinking that you will be less at risk from burglary. Burglars will often start at the top of a block and work their way down towards their escape route, so beware.

For convenience, most communal access doors are fitted with locks that can be unlocked automatically from each flat. The level of access control required will depend on the number of flats in the block, and three typical situations are covered here.

Up to three flats Normally, access control measures would not be necessary in buildings containing up to three flats (other than actually having a street door), especially if they occupied the ground and first floors. This would enable you to use a rim lock and a BS 3621 mortice deadlock (with an internal operating knob) on the door, giving two points of locking instead of the single point provided by a remotely released lock. If you and your neighbours felt it necessary to be able to communicate with a caller before going to the door, you could have an audio link installed between the flats and the communal door.

It might be necessary to make an exception if a disabled person occupied the ground floor, since a system that allowed remote door release would be a necessity rather than a luxury. In this situation, you could even consider a full audio-visual access control system, which would enable the disabled person to talk to and see a caller.

Up to nine flats Where a common entrance serves up to nine flats, or where there is a flat on a second floor, a remote door release with an audio link to each flat would be a sensible choice.

Ten or more flats While the police encourage architects of new developments to keep the number of flats served by a communal door to no more than ten, there are many existing blocks where that limit is exceeded. If you are in this situation, you would benefit from a full audio-visual access control system.

Recently, in some very large blocks of flats, the owners – private, local authority and housing association – have taken this a step further by building reception areas and employing door staff to control access into the block. This is known as a 'concierge' and, in effect, creates a reception area not unlike the type you would find in a hotel.

THE EFFECTIVENESS OF ACCESS CONTROL

Access control will help prevent trespass into the communal parts of a building and reduce the risk of burglary through private flat entrance doors. However, the inherent value will be reduced if:

- Visitors are allowed to walk in behind residents.

- Residents allow admission to unknown callers.

- There is a tradesperson door release button.

- There is a need to deliver milk, newspapers and post to the private flat doors, and to read utility meters.

- Residents within the block are the source of the problem.

TRADESPERSON RELEASE BUTTON

Tradesperson release buttons provide opportunities for a significant proportion of burglaries in flats. It is a folly to install a high-quality communal entrance door, only to allow access to all and sundry, sometimes up to 1pm each day. If these buttons are required, they should operate between 6am and 10am only (when most burglars tend to be tucked up in bed) – although this must be cleared with the Royal Mail.

To minimise the number of entries through a communal door by delivery workers and others, the police support the use of security letter boxes, which can be accessed from outside the building. In brand-new developments, they also like the utility meters to be placed where they can be read from outside.

Sometimes, this can be achieved by an 'airlock' system, whereby an additional access controlled door is placed farther inside the hallway to limit the extent to which meter readers and postal workers can penetrate the private areas of blocks of flats. Although this is usually only possible in newly constructed buildings, some existing blocks are also suitable. If you are interested in investigating the possibility, contact your local police crime prevention department for advice.

ACCESS CONTROL LOCKING

Some lock manufacturers and products are listed in this section, but only as a means of giving examples of the lock types that may suit your particular requirements. For further advice, visit the Police Secured by Design website or the website of the Master Locksmiths Association, or approach a locksmith directly.

For doors thicker than 44 mm (1³/4 in), you can use an electric bolt retraction mortice deadlock or an automatic deadlocking mortice latch in conjunction with a high-security electric release staple (for example, the Yale 3100 series of industrial rated staples, or ASSA's range of access control locks and strikes).

For doors that are 44 mm (1³/4 in) thick or less, consider fitting a new thicker door. If you are happy with the existing door, however, you can use an electric bolt retraction rim lock (for example, CISA) or a rim automatic deadbolt and electric staple. The single lock should be located just below the centre of the door, avoiding any frame joints.

The back door

A back door is probably the one door that most people don't lock when they are at home. This is simply because it is in regular use and, unlike a front door, won't lock automatically when the door closes. It tends only to be locked when the house is left unoccupied or at night when everyone goes to bed. Another reason that back doors remain unlocked is that most people would consider their back gardens to be relatively secure and wouldn't fear someone just walking in through the door. Burglars know this, so if you want to be one step ahead, get into the habit of turning the key in the sash lock each time you close the door from the inside.

BASIC REQUIREMENTS

The door Your back door should be at least 44 mm (1³/4 in) thick.

The frame The frame should be secured to a brick wall with screws or frame fixers at maximum centres of 600 mm (2 ft) and 300 mm (1 ft) from each corner. If the wall is constructed from aerated concrete blocks, or if you think the risk of burglary is particularly high, reduce this to 450-mm (1 ft 6-in) centres.

Hinges The door should hang on three hinges.

Hinge bolts Irrespective of the opening

direction of the door, fit a pair of hinge bolts, 150 mm (6 in) below the top hinge and 150 mm above the bottom hinge.
Mortice sash lock A BS 3621 mortice sash lock with boxed keep should be fitted just below the centre of the door, avoiding any timber joints
Mortice security bolts A pair of mortice security bolts should be installed at the top and bottom of the door in the stile,

operating at right angles to the grain of the wood.
Plywood panels Any plywood panel that is less than about 9 mm ($^3/_8$ in) thick should be reinforced with an additional 12-mm ($^1/_2$-in) panel placed over the top, being glued and screwed to the face of the frame. Alternatively, some designs of BS PAS24 door make suitable back doors and cover all these points.

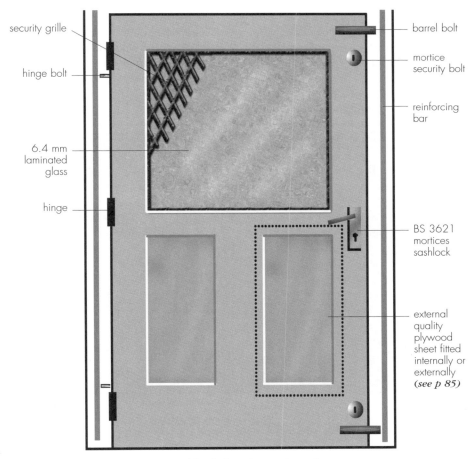

security grille

hinge bolt

6.4 mm laminated glass

hinge

barrel bolt

mortice security bolt

reinforcing bar

BS 3621 mortices sashlock

external quality plywood sheet fitted internally or externally
(see p 85)

Typical back door (internal view)

ADDITIONAL SECURITY

Barrel bolts You can fit barrel bolts on the door for night use, but read the guidance notes carefully.

Security grille On a glazed door, prevent anyone from breaking the glass to reach the locks at night by fitting a security grille inside the glazed panel or panels.

Laminated glass Ordinary glass can be replaced with 6.4- or 6.8-mm laminated glass, which will delay a burglar. Bed the glass on glazing mastic, and secure it by gluing and pinning the glazing beads.

Reinforcing bars If the back door opens inwards, reinforce the frame by fitting Birmingham bars to its inner face on both sides.

Wooden French doors

These double doors come in a variety of glazing designs, ranging from a single pane of glass per door to as many as ten. Although it is difficult to say which design is most secure, the four-pane style seems to be most at risk. This type of door provides a pane of glass that can be kicked out on to the carpet inside to leave an opening large enough to crawl through. Large single panes present a safety and noise problem for the burglar, while a ten-pane door offers an opening through which only the tiniest of burglars could crawl. Having said that, burglars have been known to work with children. The child is passed through a small open

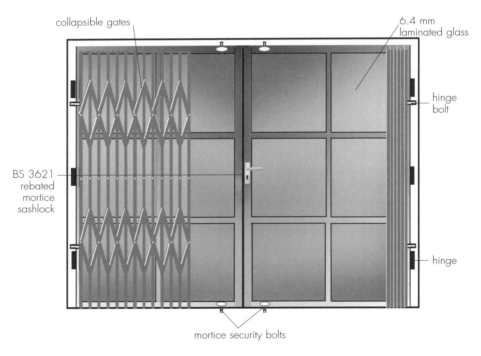

collapsible gates

6.4 mm laminated glass

hinge bolt

BS 3621 rebated mortice sashlock

hinge

mortice security bolts

Typical timber French doors (internal view)

IT'S A DOG'S LIFE

Coming to the end of a home security survey, a crime prevention officer (CPO) asked the householder if he had any concerns about the security of his back door. 'No Officer, nothing that springs to mind,' came the reply. When the CPO went into the kitchen, however, he saw a dog flap in the door. He was amazed at its size and thought he would demonstrate how easy it would be for a man to crawl through from outside. He got about half-way through when the man's dog – a handsome bull-mastiff – decided to come in from the garden. Pulling his trousers up in casualty after the tetanus injection, the CPO swore that he would refrain from playing dog in the future. Seriously, stick to cat flaps, and remember that even one of these can be reached through with an arm or tool to manipulate a lock, so don't leave the key in the lock.

window or a broken pane of glass and then runs off to find the keys inside to let the adult in. Very soon, it will be possible to buy replacement French doors that meet the requirements of PAS24. Visit the Secured by Design website for the latest news.

BASIC REQUIREMENTS

The door Your French doors should be at least 44 mm (1³/₄ in) thick.

The frame The frame should be secured to a brick wall with screws or frame fixers at maximum centres of 600 mm (2 ft) and 300 mm (1 ft) from each corner. If the wall is constructed from aerated concrete blocks, or if you think the risk of burglary is particularly high, reduce this to 450-mm (1 ft 6-in) centres.

Hinges Each door should hang on three hinges.

Hinge bolts Irrespective of the opening direction of the doors, fit each of them with a pair of hinge bolts, 150 mm (6 in) below the top hinge and 150 mm above the bottom hinge.

Mortice sash lock A BS 3621 mortice sash lock with boxed keep should be fitted just below the centre of the first opening door, avoiding any frame joints. Depending on the construction of the doors, you may need to purchase a rebated style lock. If the existing sash lock requires upgrading, take it with you to the locksmith or DIY store to ensure that you buy the correct size of replacement. (Do leave someone in the house when you do this!)

Mortice security bolts A mortice security bolt should be installed at the top and bottom of each door, in the top and bottom rails so that they operate at right angles to the grain of the wood. You will have to take the doors off to fit them. If the mortice bolt will occupy more than half the thickness of the wood, use a surface mounted press-bolt instead.

Some doors have hand operated espagnolette bolts at the top and bottom of the leading edge of the second opening door, which are covered by the first opening door when the doors are closed. If you have these bolts, leave them in place and use them. In this case, you won't have to fit the second opening door with mortice security bolts.

Plywood panels Any plywood panel that is less than about 9 mm (³/₈ in) thick, should be reinforced with an additional 12-mm (¹/₂-in) panel placed over the top, being glued and screwed to the face of the frame. This will normally only be required on the very bottom panels if unglazed.

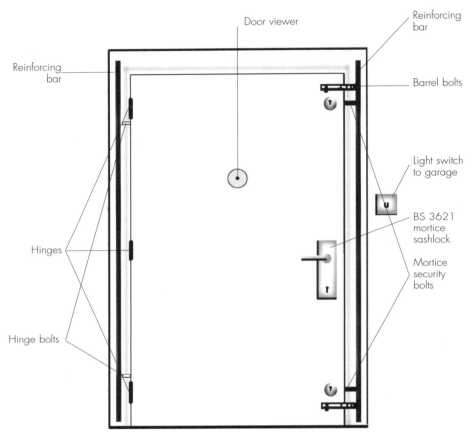

Door viewer

Reinforcing bar

Reinforcing bar

Barrel bolts

Light switch to garage

BS 3621 mortice sashlock

Mortice security bolts

Hinges

Hinge bolts

Integral garage access door (house side)

ADDITIONAL SECURITY

Laminated glass Ordinary glass can be replaced with 6.4 or 6.8 mm laminated glass, which will delay a burglar. Bed the glass on glazing mastic, and secure it by gluing and pinning the glazing beads.

Security grilles To prevent forced entry through the glass panes, fit a security grille to the inside of each door or consider installing a pair of collapsible gates.

An integral garage access door

This is a door that leads directly into the garage from the house. Almost certainly, it will be fire rated to a minimum of 30 minutes and fitted with a door closer. This type of door should be treated in the same way as an external door, because if a burglar managed to get into the garage – perhaps because you forgot to lock it –

he could work on the access door unseen from the street.

BASIC REQUIREMENTS

The door Your garage access door should be at least 44 mm (1³/4 in) thick; make sure that it is fire rated and fitted with a door closer.

The frame The frame should be secured to a brick wall with screws or frame fixers at maximum centres of 600 mm (2 ft) and 300 mm (1 ft) from each corner. If the wall is constructed from aerated concrete blocks, or if you think the risk of burglary is particularly high, reduce this to 450-mm (1 ft 6-in) centres.

Hinges The door should hang on three hinges.

Hinge bolts Irrespective of the opening direction of the door, fit a pair of hinge bolts, 150 mm (6 in) below the top hinge and 150 mm above the bottom hinge.

Mortice sash lock A BS 3621 mortice sash lock with boxed keep should be fitted just below the centre of the door, avoiding any frame joints

Door viewer Fit a door viewer at a convenient height so that you can see into garage.

Mortice security bolts Install a pair of mortice security bolts in the stiles at the top and bottom of the door, operating at right angles to the grain of the wood.

ADDITIONAL SECURITY

Barrel bolts You can fit barrel bolts on the door for night use, but read the guidance notes carefully.

Reinforcing bars If the door opens into the house, reinforce the frame by fitting Birmingham bars to its inner face on both sides. See frame reinforcing bars later in this chapter.

Sliding patio doors

Very soon, it will be possible to buy replacement sliding patio doors that meet the requirements of PAS24. Visit the Secured by Design website for the latest news. (*See also 'Sliding patio door lock', pp 82-3*)

Door locks and security hardware

RIM LOCK

Often called a night latch or 'Yale' lock, a rim lock comprises a lock body, key cylinder and keep or staple. It fits on the inner face of the door and is operated from the inside by a knob, and from the outside by a key. The bolt is spring loaded and is known as a 'live' bolt. It has a rounded shape so that you can shut the door without using the key or knob. Rim

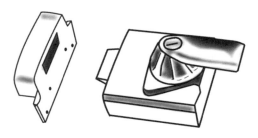

Typical rim lock

ESSENTIAL ADVICE
In the vast majority of cases, a rim lock will be used in combination with a mortice deadlock. The rim lock should be approximately one third of the door's height from the top, and the mortice deadlock approximately one third of its height from the bottom, avoiding any frame joints.

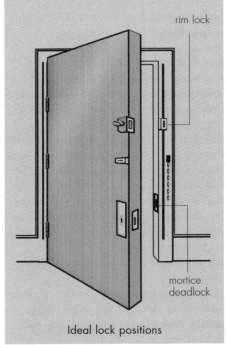

Ideal lock positions

locks vary in quality, and the price you pay will usually determine a lock's effectiveness against a burglar.

All doors need a live bolt (or latch) so that you can easily open and close the door, and although this is usually provided by a rim lock, sometimes it will be incorporated into a multi-point locking system (as often found in a PAS24 door set) or a mortice lock (a sash lock). Most rim locks have a 'lock-back' snib or slider that enables you to secure the live bolt in the locked or unlocked position. There is no security value in this; it is intended only as a means of stopping the door from locking you out when you need to carry something through.

The more secure types of rim lock incorporate a spring loaded pin in addition to, or as part of, the live bolt, which automatically deadlocks the live bolt when the door is closed. This prevents the live bolt from being slipped back by forcing a piece of plastic between a loose fitting door and its frame. Other rim locks can be deadlocked with the key from the outside.

The better rim locks, especially those that carry the BS 3621 Kitemark for thief-resistant locks, have a locking knob as well, which you can lock using its own cylinder as you go out, or by a double turn of the outside cylinder. The knob is unlocked using the outside cylinder. Only use this facility when your home is unoccupied so that you don't accidentally lock somebody inside. There are two reasons for locking the internal knob: to prevent a burglar from breaking the glass and using the knob to open the door, and to make the successful burglar leave your home by the same route that he entered.

When buying a new rim lock, make sure that it is British Standard Kitemarked. Such locks are designed to resist attack by drilling the cylinder, sawing the live bolt and otherwise forcing the mechanism. There will also be a minimum of a thousand key differs, but since they all use cylinders, the actual key differs will number many thousands. Make sure you buy a lock that is handed correctly (depending on whether the door is hinged on the right or left) and that its size matches the stile width of the door. The main weakness of the rim lock is the installation, especially that of the keep. Make sure that you use the longest screws possible to fit both lock and keep.

MORTICE DEADLOCK

The mortice deadlock, which is normally used on front doors and private flat entrance doors, is fitted into a slot (mortice) cut into the leading edge of a door. Mortice deadlocks are available in two body sizes for standard-width and narrow door stiles. The deadbolt, which is operated by a key and a levered locking mechanism or a cylinder, engages into a keep set into the door frame. A door fitted with such a lock should have a minimum thickness of 44 mm ($1^3/4$ in) and be in good condition. There is a wide range of mortice locks, and the cost is likely to determine quality. At the very least, you should use a BS 3621 Kitemarked mortice deadlock for the final exit door, and for any door to an outbuilding that contains items of value. A BS 3621 mortice lock will

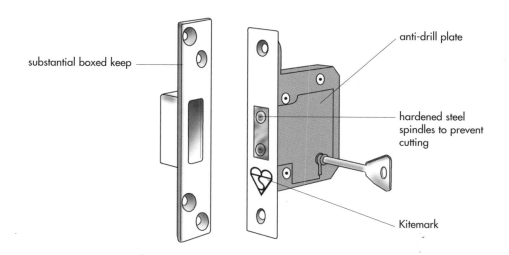

substantial boxed keep

anti-drill plate

hardened steel spindles to prevent cutting

Kitemark

A BS 3621 mortice deadlock

How to fit a mortice deadlock

A choice way of making a door secure is to fit a top quality mortice lock. With a mortice being defined as "a rectangular hole", a mortice lock is one that fits inside a mortice or hole. If you enjoy basic DIY, then fitting this type of lock is a good, swift low-cost option.

TOOLS AND MATERIALS

- Top quality BS mortice lock
- Pencil and measuring rule
- Marking gauge
- Try square
- Bevel edged chisel at 19 mm wide
- Mallet
- Electric drill

- Flat drill bits: 12 mm and 19 mm
- Small twist drill bit for pilot holes
- Spike or awl for marking
- Keyhole or pad saw
- Masking tape
- Screwdrivers to fit your chosen screws

1 MARKING THE POSITION OF THE LOCK
Set the body of the mortice lock flat and flush against the edge of the door so that it is 50 mm below the central horizontal member. Use a pencil to carefully mark in the position of the mortice hole on the edge of the door.

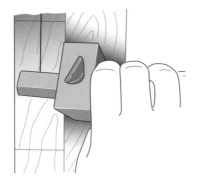

2 MARKING THE MORTICE
Set the marking gauge to half the thickness of the door and scribe a line down the centre of the edge. Use the pencil, square and gauge to mark in the precise length and width of the mortice hole.

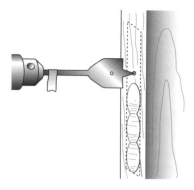

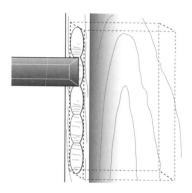

3 DRILLING THE HOLES

Fit the drill with the 19 mm flat bit. Use a piece of masking tape to mark the drill bit so that you know when the drilled holes are slightly deeper than the length of the body of the lock. Set the point of the drill on the scribed centre line, and drill 4 to 5 linked holes into the thickness of the door.

4 CHISELLING OUT THE MORTICE

Take the bevel edged chisel and mallet, and little by little cut away the waste from around the drilled holes until you have a mortice hole that is big enough to take the body of the lock. With the lock fitted in the mortice, mark around the plate with a pencil. Use the chisel to pare out a recess for the plate so that the plate finishes flush with the edge of the door.

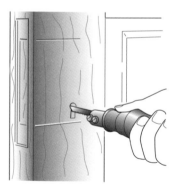

5 MARKING THE KEYHOLE

Use the spike to mark in the position of the keyhole. Centre the 12 mm flat drill bit on the mark and run a hole through into the mortice, first from one side of the door and then from the other.

6 CUTTING THE KEYHOLE

Insert the keyhole or pad saw into the 12 mm drilled hole and cut a slot big enough to take the key, first on one side of the door then on the other. Slide the body of the lock into the mortice, drill pilot holes for the various screws and fix into place. Fit the plate over the keyhole. Finally, fit the striking plate into the doorframe. Mark around it with a pencil, drill and chisel out a recess for the striking bolt and screw into position.

also be supplied with a boxed keep, which is cut into the door frame, rather than being a simple plate with a hole in it.

Unfortunately, many European manufactured locks will not carry a BS 3621 Kitemark. This does not necessarily mean that they should be replaced, as some offer a level of security that either matches or exceeds the requirements of that standard. In this situation, the best thing to do is ask the advice of a locksmith before you go to the expense of replacing it. If you have to remove the lock to do this, make sure you leave somebody at home. Check also that your insurer is happy about you using the lock, even if the locksmith tells you it's the best thing since sliced bread.

MORTICE SASH LOCK

A mortice sash lock combines the actions of a rim lock and a mortice deadlock in one unit, incorporating a live bolt (or latch) that is operated by a handle on each side of the door. The same BS 3621 standard applies to these locks, which are normally fitted to back doors and internal garage access doors. This type of lock is normally fitted just below the centre of a door, so mortice security bolts will be

A BS 3621 mortice sash lock

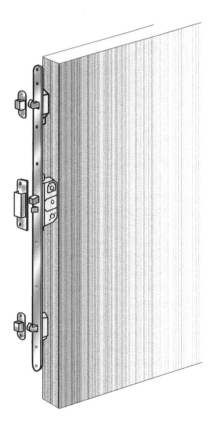

Typical multi-point locking mechanism

needed at the top and bottom of the door to reduce the amount of leverage that can be applied against the lock.

MULTI-POINT LOCKING

In recent years, many homes have had their doors and windows replaced by double-glazed plastic and aluminium units. Most of these will have multi-point locking.

As a rule, a multi-point locking system has at least one hook lock, which engages with a keep in the frame and will resist a lever attack on the door. There will be at least two compression bolts that pull the door tight against the draught seals and contribute to the security of the door, and there will be a live bolt close to the operating handle so that you can open and close the door easily. Some systems also have additional bolts that shoot into the top and bottom frames, and the most secure versions have bolts that engage into the frame on the hinge side of the door.

In most cases, the hook locks, compression bolts and shoot bolts are engaged by lifting the handle. Then the key has to be turned in the cylinder lock to deadlock the bolts in place. This can be done from inside or outside of door. More recent types automatically engage some or all of the elements of the multi-point locking system when the door is closed.

A multi-point locking system will vary depending on the location of the door and its precise purpose. For example, the outside handle of a front door fitted to a typical two-storey house normally would only be used to engage the various security bolts, but wouldn't operate the live bolt. This means that you would need the key to get back into the house each time you closed the front door, just like a

Mortice security bolt

door fitted with a rim lock. Of course, you could easily lock yourself out in these circumstances, which is a good reason to leave a spare key with a trusted neighbour or friend. Private entrance doors to flats above the ground floor, which open off an internal corridor (where there are seldom any windows to break should you lock yourself out), will have an outside handle that operates the live bolt as well as the other security bolts.

MORTICE SECURITY BOLT

Sometimes called a mortice rack bolt, the mortice security bolt provides additional security for doors that have been fitted with a mortice sashlock. It is more secure than an ordinary surface mounted barrel bolt, because it is key operated and fits into a mortice. This type of fitting should

be installed in pairs, at the top and bottom of wooden back or side doors, French doors and internal garage access doors. The unit comprises a bolt within a cylindrical case that fits tightly into a hole (mortice) drilled into the edge of the door frame across the grain. Thus, the bolt operates horizontally in single doors and vertically on double doors, shooting into a hole in the top or side of the door frame, or in the sill beneath the door. Mortice security bolts use a common splined key, which could easily be carried by a burglar. However, these bolts are only operated from the inside (there's no keyhole on the outside), and unless a burglar broke through a door panel or glazing to reach the lock, he would not be able to take advantage of having a key.

For fire safety, these bolts should not be

set at night. They should only be used to reinforce the security of your doors when you leave your home unoccupied. For extra security at night, employ simple barrel bolts.

BARREL BOLT

This surface mounted bolt is normally fitted to the inside of front and back doors, and is handy for providing a little extra night-time security when you're tucked up in bed. Using a large barrel bolt, together with a BS 3621 mortice sash lock or deadlock and rim lock, will provide you with a good level of security without compromising your ability to escape through the door in an emergency.

Since a barrel bolt is surface mounted, it must be attached using the longest and thickest screws that are practical for the door and fitting. This may mean rejecting the screws supplied with the bolt.

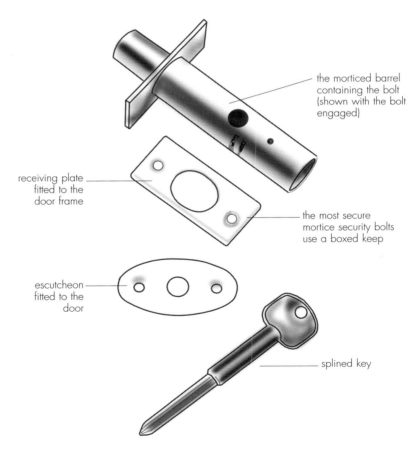

the morticed barrel containing the bolt (shown with the bolt engaged)

receiving plate fitted to the door frame

the most secure mortice security bolts use a boxed keep

escutcheon fitted to the door

splined key

Main elements of a mortice security bolt

HINGE BOLT

Also known as a dog bolt, the hinge bolt is a fixed steel bolt that is fitted in pairs to the hinge side of a wooden door. When the door is closed, the bolts engage into holes drilled in the frame. They serve two purposes. One is to prevent the door from being forced open on the hinge side – a rare event, but it does happen; the other is to prevent an outward opening door, which has exposed hinges, from being removed completely from the door frame by removing or cutting out the hinge pins. Hinge bolts should be fitted to all external wooden doors. The more expensive types have a boxed keep to receive the bolt rather than a simple steel plate with a hole in it.

It is normal practice to fit one hinge bolt about 150 mm below the top hinge and the second hinge the same distance above the bottom hinge.

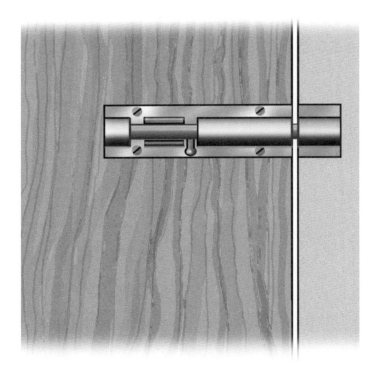

Typical barrel bolt

MORTICE LOCK REINFORCING PLATES

Cutting a lock mortice in a door frame inevitably weakens the wood. A tight fitting mortice lock will restore some of the lost strength, but if it is slightly loose, the lock could act as an internal lever and split the wood if force is applied. Mortice lock reinforcing plates, which are bolted through the door above and below the lock, sandwich the wood and lock tightly together to help prevent this from occurring during an attack. They should be fitted as a matter of course with all mortice sash locks and deadlocks.

SECURITY TIP

In recent times, locking hinges have been developed. These incorporate a pin on one side of the hinge that locks into the other side when the hinge is closed. In effect, this does exactly the same thing as a hinge bolt – even if the hinge pin is knocked out, the door remains held in the frame.

FRAME REINFORCEMENT BARS

To increase the resistance of a door frame against splitting during an attempted burglary, you can fit flat steel bars to the inner faces of the frame. These can be

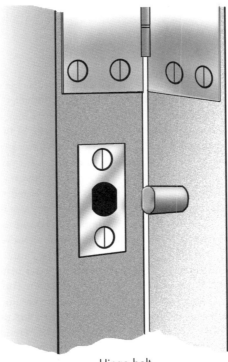

Hinge bolt

Mortice lock reinforcing plates

obtained from locksmiths and are usually painted white. The locking-side bar, often referred to as a London bar, will have to be made to measure to fit around the rim lock's striking box and any surface mounted barrel bolts that may be installed. The hinge-side bar, often referred to as a Birmingham bar, can be bought off the shelf and simply cut to length.

LETTER PLATE AND LETTER PLATE DEFLECTOR

In many cases, a burglar can reach through a letter plate with his arm or a tool to operate the knob of a rim lock or a key left in a mortice deadlock. Various tools are used for this purpose, but a looped length of electrical cable is a favourite. A recent trend in housebreaking

and car theft has become known as 'fishing rod burglary'. In this situation, a thief inserts a long rod with a hook or a large piece of Blu-Tack on the end through the letter plate, picks up the car or house keys left on the hall table, then either steals the car or lets himself in to burgle the home, or does both. This method of burglary has become quite common in recent times, so it is important to take steps to prevent it.

Fortunately, both risks are easily tackled by fitting a letter plate deflector to the back of the door. This painted steel cowl, which can be obtained from a locksmith, deflects letters and newspapers down on to the floor, but completely blocks access to locks and your hall table.

A similar solution can be achieved by

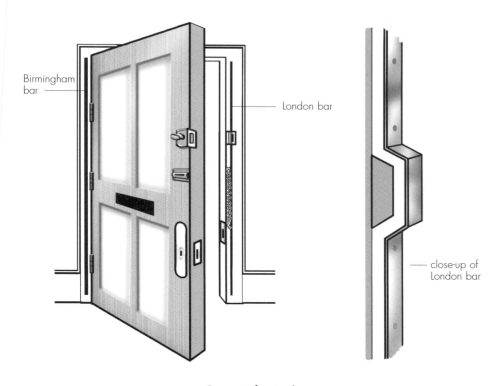

Birmingham bar

London bar

close-up of London bar

Door reinforcing bars

fitting a letter basket to the back of the door, if you have enough room. However, this does make it possible for mail to be stolen through the letter plate, so it would be better to adapt the basket so that the mail falls to the floor.

FIRE-RESISTANT POST BOX
If you are concerned about pranksters pushing fireworks through your letter plate, you can install a fire-resistant steel box on the back of the door. This acts like a letter-box, having a small flap so that you can collect your mail. This device is designed to contain a fire or any fuel, such

as petrol, that might be poured through the letter plate. Some models incorporate a heat-activated fire extinguisher. You can buy one from a master locksmith.

OPENING THE DOOR TO CALLERS
Many people, especially the elderly, are concerned about answering the door to callers, particularly late at night or when they're unexpected. Fortunately, there are a number of inexpensive door chains, limiters and viewers that provide added security when answering the front door. That said, a door is far more secure when it's closed and locked than when it's open

How to fit a letter plate deflector

We all know about the long arm of the law, but who would have thought that long-armed burglars could gain entry through our letterboxes! An effective way to stop and block this sly and slippery problem is to fit a letter plate deflector.

TOOLS AND MATERIALS

- Top quality BS metal letter plate deflector with screws to fit
- Pencil and measuring rule
- Short spirit level
- Spike or awl

- Electric drill
- Drill bits suitable for drilling holes for your chosen screws
- Screwdriver

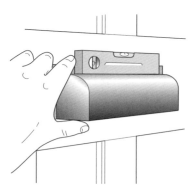

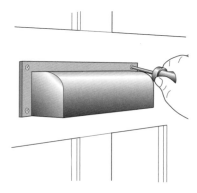

1 POSITIONING THE DEFLECTOR

Set the deflector in place on the inside of the door so that it is centred and perfectly positioned over the letterbox slot. Use the spirit level to make sure that it is level, and use the pencil to mark in the screw holes. Remove the deflector and use the spike to create centre-point locations for the drill.

2 FIXING THE DEFLECTOR

Drill pilot holes marked for the screws and use the screwdriver to fix the deflector in place on the door. Finally, make sure that the letters can still be delivered.

Typical door chain

on a door chain, so if in doubt, don't open the door. Instead, simply talk (or shout) through the door or a window, preferably one on the first floor, which you will be able to open to permit a relatively normal conversation. Whatever you do, always acknowledge a call to the door. Otherwise, if the caller is a burglar, he may assume that you're not at home and attempt an entry.

DOOR LIMITERS AND CHAINS

These devices are engaged before you open the door, preferably against your shoed foot, or a rubber or wooden wedge. They restrict the amount by which the door can be opened, allowing you to have a conversation with a caller and to accept items of identification through the gap. The police tend to recommend door limiters these days because their screw fittings are slightly stronger than those of chains. Both require the door to be closed before you can disengage them and open the door fully. This means that the caller cannot release them, and that's what

makes them security fittings.

A common mistake when using this type of device is to treat it as a door lock and have it engaged all of the time, except when opening the door to a caller, which defeats the object of having it. Remember, the chain goes on and then the door is opened.

Because this misuse is a common problem, many elderly people, particularly those living in warden controlled sheltered accommodation, have what is known as a lockable door chain. This allows the warden to unlock the device from the outside if the occupant needs help, but can't get to the door.

DOOR VIEWER AND MIRROR

A door viewer should be used in conjunction with a door limiter. Locksmiths and DIY stores sell a wide range, but the most common has a small, wide-angle lens that offers a field of view of between 160 and 180 degrees. This type of spy-hole viewer comes in two parts, which are screwed together through

A DIY DOOR WEDGE (GRANNY'S BOOT)

An old way of controlling the opening of the door is with a wooden wedge fixed to the bottom of a broom handle, affectionately known as a 'Granny's boot'. The handle removes the need to bend down to position the wedge under the door. In theory, the harder you push the door against the wedge, the more stuck it will become. However, its effectiveness will be determined by the roughness of the floor surface and the roughness of the bottom of the wedge. A wedge can be cut from softwood and its bottom face given a toothed profile to ensure maximum grip on carpet. For a hard floor surface, you could try gluing a piece of rubber to the underside of the wedge. This device should only be used in conjunction with a door chain or limiter.

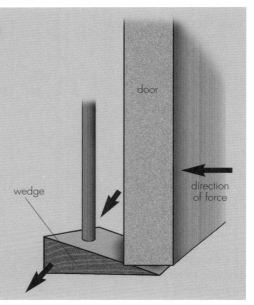

Typical door limiter

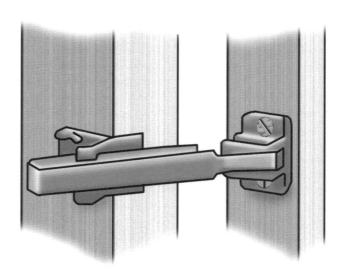

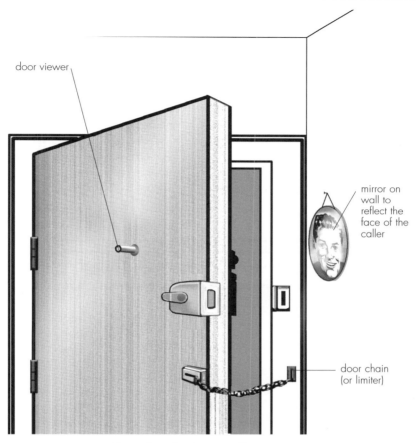

door viewer

mirror on
wall to
reflect the
face of the
caller

door chain
(or limiter)

Controlling the door to callers

a hole drilled in the door. The inner part has a small cover to prevent light in the hall from leaking out through the door. Spectacle wearers can find these small viewers laborious to use, since most remove their spectacles to look through them. These days, however, you can buy viewers with much larger lenses. Some types take the form of a simple tube through the door, with a diameter of about 10 mm (^{3}/8 in), and have a mirrored outer cover to prevent anyone from looking through it from the outside. The very latest viewers employ a prism to project an image of the caller on to a small screen about 30 mm (1^1/4 in) in diameter. At night, all of them require an outside light or a lit corridor to be effective.

As an alternative, or preferably an addition, to the door viewer, you can fit a small make-up mirror to the wall on the locking side of the door. If set at a slight angle, this will enable you to see a caller when you open the door on the limiter.

SLIDING PATIO DOOR LOCK

Patio door locks are available to supplement the poor locking mechanisms often fitted to older sliding patio doors. Amazingly, during the 1970s, some of the cheapest aluminium sliding doors (and windows) were supplied with plastic catches only, and little effort was needed to lift the doors from their tracks. Today, most doors of this type are provided with multi-point locking systems that include hook bolts to pull the door into the frame and prevent it from being lifted.

A patio door lock is normally fitted to the bottom portion of the frame, immediately next to the fixed door or to the stile of the fixed door, whichever is most convenient. For even greater security, a second lock can be fitted to the top of the frame. It is best to fit the lock either on or up against the fixed door, as any force applied to slide open the door will push

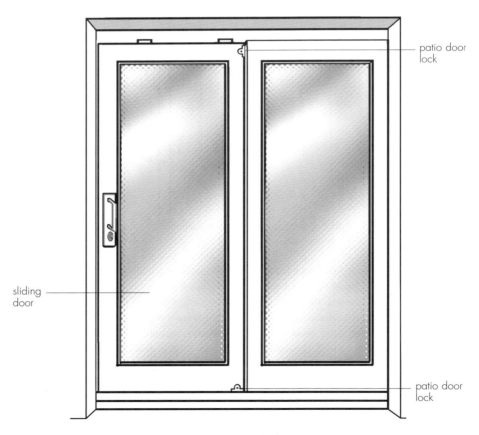

patio door lock

sliding door

patio door lock

Patio door locks

the lock into its fitting. If the lock is fitted to the other side, there is a danger that it will be pulled from its fitting.

RECESSED DOOR

A recessed door can encourage loitering and anti-social behaviour. In particular, it offers opportunities for the burglar, who can hide in the recess while forcing open the door. However, most recessed doors are outward opening (usually to aid escape in an emergency), which means that they are difficult to force in against the doorstops and therefore can help reduce the opportunity for burglary. The fact that they are outward opening is usually the reason why they are recessed, since it is not permissible for doors to open across a public footway or highway.

In many cases, a recessed doorway can be brought forward provided due regard is given to the requirements of relevant legislation and regulation. By and large, these relate to the safety of the building's occupants in the event of an emergency such as a fire, and the safety and convenience of individuals on the footway or highway outside.

WHAT YOU CAN DO ABOUT A RECESSED DOOR

The following are three possible solutions to a recessed door that presents a security problem.

Solution 1 Remove the recess by bringing the door forward.

Normally, this can be achieved if there are no more than 60 users of the emergency exit doors, including the entrance door, since this figure allows the doors to open inwards.

If there is a private forecourt in front of the door of sufficient size, the door can be brought forward to open on to the forecourt. To ensure the safety of pedestrians, some form of structure must be placed on each side of the door opening arc. This could take the form of an area of small cobbles, a deflector rail on the wall, a planter, a bollard or a rail.

Although not a requirement under the Building Regulations, it is a good idea to include a glazed panel in an outward opening door, as this allows the user to see if there is an obstruction (or a pedestrian) on the other side. Use laminated glass with a small-gauge security grille fixed behind it. These measures will help to prevent a burglar from operating

Bringing a recessed door forward

the 'crash' bars or other emergency release mechanism by breaking the viewing panel. If the door needs to be of a fire- and smoke-resistant type, the building control officer will advise you.

If the recess has an inward opening door, which is more susceptible to being kicked in than an outward opening door, you must ensure that the door and its locking provision will satisfy both the security and fire safety needs. Consulting your insurer is also a wise move. Visit the Secured by Design website for details of manufacturers who can supply high-security doors (PAS24) that will also meet the necessary fire safety requirements.

Solution 2 Reduce the depth of the recess to a minimum

If it is not possible to bring the door forward to the very front of the recess, make sure that the depth of the recess is no greater than that needed to open the door within it. Where possible, try to achieve a recess depth of no more than 600 mm (2 ft).

A local authority may allow a slight projection over the highway on the understanding that a particular door will rarely be used. Wall mounted deflectors or other structures may be required. The resulting shallow recess can be made less encouraging of anti-social behaviour by taking steps to improve observation of it from outside.

A few other measures are also worth considering, particularly if you have problems with drug users. Thoroughly clean the recess and repair holes in the walls, ceiling and floor surfaces. Paint the walls and ceiling with anti-graffiti paint. This will make it easier to remove any new graffiti or marks. If there is a great deal of informal observation of the recess, such as lots of people walking by, paint the walls and ceiling a light colour and install a bright light. If the door is solid, fit a glazed panel as described in Solution 1. Alternatively, install a viewer so that any user can look out into the recess before opening the door.

Solution 3 Using shutters and gates

Security shutters that rise automatically when a fire alarm is activated are sometimes permissible, but this depends very much on the situation. Those that have been accepted by the fire service in London have been mains powered, with a battery back-up in case of mains failure. They also have a fail-safe winding mechanism to cope with a total power failure.

REINFORCING PLYWOOD PANELS

Most references for the need to strengthen thin plywood panels indicate that an additional 12-mm sheet of external-grade plywood be fitted over the top on the outside of the door. There is no reason why it cannot be fitted internally and is therefore a matter of personal preference.

USEFUL CONTACTS

ASSA Abloy Group
www.abloysecurity.co.uk

Association of British Insurers (The)
www.abi.org.uk

British Security Industry Association (The)
www.bsia.co.uk

CISA
www.cisa.com

Crime Prevention Products
www.c-p-p.co.uk

Crime Reduction
www.crimereduction.gov.uk

Domestic Mailbox
www.domesticmailbox.com

Loss Prevention Certification Board (The)
www.brecertification.co.uk

Mailboxes Direct
www.mailboxesdirect.co.uk

Postbox Shop
www.postboxshop.co.uk

Secured by Design
www.securedbydesign.com

Yale Security Systems
www.yale.co.uk

Window security

You may think that even if you do secure your windows with locks that a burglar would simply break through the glass. Fortunately, when given the choice, most burglars would rather not smash out a window pane and climb through the resultant mess. Breaking through glass takes time and, importantly, makes quite a lot of noise, increasing the risk of discovery. The major problem for a burglar in this situation, however, is the strong possibility that he might leave valuable forensic evidence behind him, such as fingerprints, clothing fibres, shoe prints and blood (leading to DNA). Moreover, microscopic shards of glass will be trapped in his clothing and can be matched to those of the window, tying him directly to the offence. Making a burglar use a tool to force open a window can further help the forensic scientists, as they are often able to match the marks it leaves to those found at the scenes of other burglaries and to the tool itself. In other words, a well-locked window will help to prevent a crime from occurring in the first place, and if it does fail and the burglar breaks through the glass, the chances are that he will be tracked down after the event.

There are three methods of breaking through a window: forcing it open with a lever – made much easier when no locks are fitted; breaking through the glass; and, particularly with some replacement double-glazed windows, removing the entire frame. That said, a surprising 15 per cent of burglaries (some 200,000 each year) involve no forcing at all – the burglar simply opens an unlocked door

or climbs through an open window!

There's an enormous range of window locks designed for every type of window and most window materials, and you'll find exactly what you're looking for at a locksmith's or large DIY store. The vast majority are very easy to fit, so there are no excuses for insecure windows. This chapter covers the most common types, although there are some specialised locks for aluminium and plastic double-glazed windows that will only be available from a locksmith.

The majority of window locks use common keys. In other words, one key will open an entire range of locks. This is not a problem because to gain access to the lock, the burglar has to smash the glass, and if he's done that, he might as well come through it rather than waste time fiddling with the window lock. Moreover, different ranges have different common keys, and because there are so many to choose from, a burglar would have to carry a large bunch to cover all eventualities. Special locking and opening devices for doors and windows belonging to the disabled can be obtained through a master locksmith.

High-security windows

Chapter 4 looked at the British Standards Institution's product assessment specification for enhanced door security (PAS 24). The window security standard is pretty much the same apart from the fact that it has been developed to a full British Standard Kitemark – BS 7950: 1997. At the time of writing, however, sliding sash windows are not included within

SECURITY TIP
If you're on a tight budget and there are some windows that you never open, you can always screw them permanently closed. Use angle brackets or joint blocks for wooden casement windows, self-tapping screws for metal windows, and brass screws in brass screw cups for sliding sashes. Always use the longest and thickest screws appropriate for the dimensions of the frames. However, make sure that every room in your home has at least one large window fitted with locks that can be opened in an emergency.

the standard, and you should visit the Secured by Design website for the very latest information, where you will also find details of a large range of suppliers. The Kitemarked windows will have undergone a similar range of tests as the PAS 24 door sets.

A BS 7950 window fitted with 6.4-mm laminated glass and multi-point locking, with key operation in the opening handle, offers a high degree of protection against burglary, but as with door sets, it is essential to realise that the tests and the Kitemark cover the whole window and not individual components, such as the locks or hinges, so beware of misleading claims.

If you have moved into a new home in the past five years that has gained the police Secured by Design award, the chances are that the ground-floor windows and any others that are accessible by climbing will be BS 7950 Kitemarked, or at least have been tested to this standard. Although the Association of British Insurers (ABI) and its members, and other insurers who are not ABI members,

recognise the standard, you must check with your own insurer to satisfy yourself that your windows meet the minimum security standards set by the company.

WHICH WINDOWS SHOULD MEET THE STANDARD?
If it means saving a little money on replacement windows, you can restrict the use of BS 7950 windows to those that are on the ground floor, on an open balcony access, on a shared roof terrace or roof garden, or otherwise accessible by climbing. These windows should have key operation of the locks (which will almost certainly be a multi-point locking system with the key cylinder in the handle) and be glazed with a minimum of 6.4-mm laminated glass on the inner pane.

Recent changes to the Building Regulations require that at least one window of appropriate size in each habitable room (not bathrooms, hallways or kitchens) must be available for emergency escape and must not be fitted with a key operated lock. So, instead of a key on the operating handle, you'll find a simple button, which must be pressed before you can turn the handle. In these circumstances, any glazing must be laminated to 6.4 mm minimum thickness. This change won't affect you unless you have new windows installed or you move to a brand-new house. For safety, consider having opening restrictors on windows above the ground floor.

If safety glass is required for any of the windows, make sure that you use the laminated-glass equivalent for the inner pane. The outer pane can be toughened, but note that toughened glass is not a security glass (see pp 100–3).

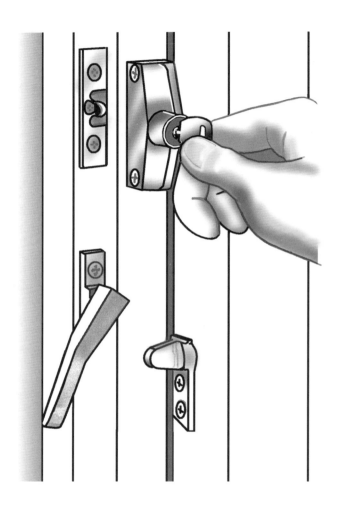

Automatic casement window lock

Casement windows

A casement window has a fixed frame and one or more side- or top-hinged opening frames (casements). Each casement should be fitted with at least one key operated casement window lock. This should be positioned just above or below a centrally mounted window catch. A small fanlight (top-hinged) window should also be locked.

On a window that is greater than 1 m (3 ft 3 in) in width or height, or for increased security (particularly on a rear or side ground-floor window), fit a pair of locks, one opposite each hinge. Use two locks on the fanlight if the window is in a vulnerable position.

Steel and aluminium windows can be fitted with purpose made, surface mounted metal window locks in the same numbers and positions. When fitting locks to double-glazed windows, take care not to break the glass with the drill bit or self-tapping screws. Metal windows (particularly steel types) can also be fitted with cockspur handle locks. This type fits just below the cockspur handle to prevent it from being opened.

Plastic windows without multi-point locking mechanisms are a little more challenging to secure. For a retrofit lock to have any real strength, it must be secured through the plastic and into the inner steel framework. Before attempting to fit locks to plastic windows, contact their supplier or manufacturer for advice and to find out if your proposed security improvement would affect any warranty that came with them. If you are not confident about fitting locks to plastic windows, employ a locksmith.

There are three basic types of window lock for ordinary casement windows: automatic, press-button and swing locks. Sometimes, they are called 'frame-to-frame' locks because each comprises two parts, one being attached to the opening frame and the other to the fixed frame.

AUTOMATIC LOCK

The easiest type of window lock to use is the style that locks automatically when you close the window; you only need a key when you want to unlock it. With an automatic lock, if you're in a rush to go out, all you have to do is close the window to be certain that it's secure.

PRESS-BUTTON LOCK

This is another easy lock, only requiring you to press in a button to engage it. To unlock the window, you need a key, but only if you've pressed the button.

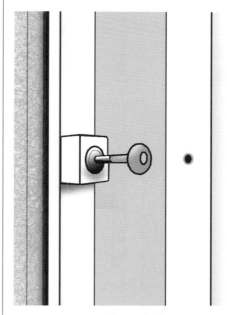

Press button lock

SWING LOCK

This type of lock has a hinged bar on the casement that swings over a tab attached to the fixed frame; normally, it is tightened in place with a key. Although time consuming to use, a swing lock does pull the casement tightly into the frame, offering the benefit of improved draughtproofing! Unfortunately, this type of lock is not suitable if you suffer from

Swing lock

arthritis or some other disability that makes using your hands difficult. In this situation, you would be better off with an automatic or push-button lock, which normally requires only a quarter-turn of the key to unlock.

Flush fitting casement windows

Some large, older houses have very big casement windows. In these, the opening frames may be flush with the fixed frames, rather than being set back into them, which is the normal arrangement. This makes it difficult to use some swing locks and automatic locks. Fortunately, these windows can be fitted with window mortice security bolts, which are installed into the leading edge of the opening frame at right angles to the grain of the wood. Two are required for really big windows.

WINDOW MORTICE SECURITY BOLT

This is a smaller version of the door mortice security bolt, which is often called a window mortise rack bolt. These locks provide a good level of security for very large, flush casements. They are normally fitted in pairs, one at the top and one at the bottom of the window, opposite the hinges. Each unit comprises a bolt within a cylindrical case, which fits tightly into a hole (mortice) drilled at right angles to the grain of the wood. Normally, it is fitted into the opening frame, and the bolt shoots into the fixed frame. However, there is no reason why it can't be installed the other way around, especially if the fixed frame is of a larger section than the opening casement. They can operate either vertically or horizontally. Mortise security bolts use a common splined key, which could easily be carried by a burglar. However, these bolts can only be operated from the inside (there's no keyhole on the outside) and unless a burglar broke through the glass to reach the lock, he would not be able to

Window mortice security bolt

A pivot or semaphore lock

take advantage of having a key. If you are concerned about this possibility, you can buy a key cylinder that fits into and covers the splined keyhole.

PIVOT LOCK

As an alternative to the mortice security bolt, you can fit a flush pivot, or semaphore, lock. As a rule, this is fitted to the opening frame and secures the window with a hardened steel bolt that drops over the fixed frame with a movement that resembles an old-fashioned railway signal. Some of these locks employ a keep, attached to the fixed frame, for a little extra security. The bolt is engaged either by turning a catch or using a key.

Leaded lights

If your windows have traditional leaded lights (small pieces of glass held together by strips of lead), you should still fit locks, but understand that it is easy to break through this type of glazing without making much noise. It may be possible to have security grilles made for the most common diamond-design leaded lights, which will be hidden behind the lead strips, but these will be expensive. You could also consider secondary glazing using laminated glass. If you are not keen on these physical solutions, consider having an alarm installed.

Sliding sash windows

The sliding sash window is very common, comprising two glazed frames (sashes) that slide up and down within an outer frame. To make light work of sliding the sashes, each is attached by cords to counterweights that run up and down inside the hollow sides of the outer frame.

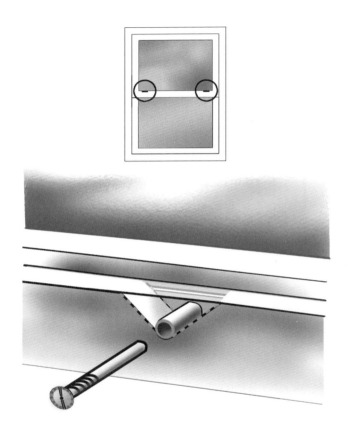

Dual screw fitted to a sliding sash window

Unfortunately, age and poor maintenance lead to a lot of these windows not sliding very well. When in good condition and correctly locked, they can slow the progress of a burglar or even deter him completely.

Sash windows suffer from a number of security weaknesses, but nothing that can't be easily remedied. Many are not fitted with key locks, relying solely on a pivoting catch that bolts the sashes together where their frames meet in the centre of the window. In some cases, it is possible to insert a thin blade of some sort between the two sashes from the outside to knock the bolt across.

Some sash windows simply don't close properly due to a build-up of paint, or distortion caused by the swelling or shrinking of the timber. This can result in gaps above or below the sashes that are large enough to allow insertion of a substantial lever, such as a spade or crowbar. Too much paint and distortion can also prevent certain types of lock from functioning.

Sash windows can be secured by three basic types of window lock: the dual screw, lockable sash stop and frame-to-frame fixing.

DUAL SCREWS

Most dual screws comprise a part-threaded bolt, which screws through an internally-threaded barrel located in the top rail of the inner (lower) sash. As the bolt is screwed in, its plain end passes into the bottom rail of the outer (upper) sash, preventing the sashes from sliding past each other. The cheapest (and most common) type of dual screw simply passes through a keep plate and into a hole drilled in the outer sash, whereas the more expensive type has a completely threaded bolt that screws into an additional threaded barrel in the outer sash. It is not uncommon for the part-threaded bolts of the cheaper types to bend or break through the rail when great leverage is applied to the bottom sash.

Another disadvantage of the dual screw is that sash windows have a tendency to swell and shrink slightly during the year, which can make aligning the components difficult. It's also possible to cut through the bolt by inserting a thin hacksaw blade between the sashes, although this rarely happens. The main problem usually lies with the fitting, however, especially when the keep plate is not used on the outer sash, because this makes it easier to force the bolt right through the rail.

If you want to use dual screws on modern sliding sash windows, which also tilt inwards for cleaning, and run up and down on metal sliders, you will have to fit the all-threaded type. This lock will prevent the window from going up and down and tilting inwards.

SASH STOPS

Equally common as the dual screw, and arguably more secure than the cheaper varieties, is the lockable sash stop. This is fitted in pairs to the stiles of the outer sash; when the removable or retractable bolts are engaged, they prevent the sashes from passing each other. They can be fitted around 100 mm (4 in) above the top rail of the inner sash (when the sashes are closed) so that the window can be opened a little for ventilation while remaining locked. To prevent damage to the tops of the stiles of the inner sash by

Lockable sash stop

93

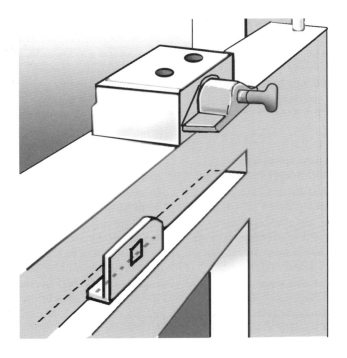

Frame to frame sash lock

the bolts, metal plates are usually supplied. Some Victorian and Georgian sashes, however, often have a decorative finish to the tops of the stiles, making it difficult, if not impossible, to fit the plates. Vulnerable windows should be fitted with two pairs of sash stops or two pairs of locking points: one to lock the window in the closed position, and the other to allow the window to be opened partially for ventilation. The latter should only be done when someone is home; if you go out, lock all windows closed.

There are two basic types of lockable sash stop. One comprises a threaded barrel that is inserted into the outer sash, allowing a pin or stop to be screwed into it with a key. The other is a one-piece lock, which is morticed into the outer sash and incorporates a bolt that can be extended or retracted, again with a key. It's similar to the mortice security bolt, but a lot smaller.

FRAME-TO-FRAME LOCK

Sashes can also be secured with a two-piece frame-to-frame lock. One part of the lock fits on to the top rail of the inner sash, while the other part is attached to the bottom rail of the outer sash. The two

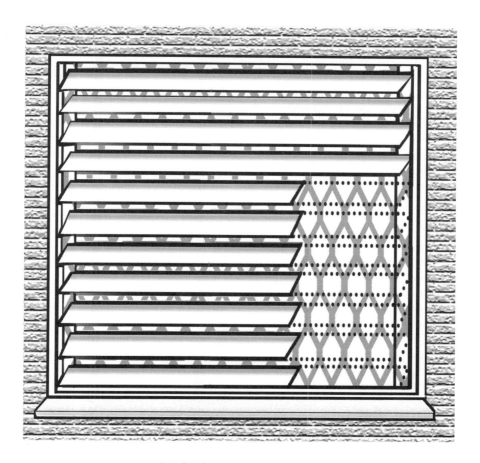

Louvre window fitted with interior fitted diamond grille

are locked together with a push-in bolt or a levered bar, both of which require a key to unlock them. The disadvantage of this type of fitting is that the gap between a pair of loose fitting sashes would allow the lock to be reached from the outside. However, they are useful if fitted in combination with dual screws or lockable sash stops, especially on modern sash windows that tilt for cleaning.

Louvre windows

These windows consist of narrow blades of glass set into aluminium or plastic frames, which open and close like a Venetian blind. Over time, the blades of glass in aluminium-framed windows may become loose in their frames, and by bending the aluminium a little, a burglar can lift the glass out. While the more modern plastic types are a little more

95

secure, the glass blades can easily be snapped in half and pulled from the frames. There is little that can be done to make a window of this type more secure, other than fitting a fixed security grille behind it. A better option would be to replace the louvre unit with a fixed pane of 6.4-mm laminated glass, using the largest possible glazing beads, which should be glued and pinned in place. Better still would be to replace it completely with a new fixed or casement window.

Ventilation at night

Many people can't sleep soundly at night unless they leave a bedroom window open – even in winter. If you are one of them, only open a fanlight window (the small top-hung casement) and install a fixed security grille behind it. Then you can leave the window open at night without fear of someone attempting to break in. Don't forget to close the window when you go out.

French windows

See 'French doors', Chap 3.

Security grilles, gates and shutters

To improve the physical security of your doors and windows beyond the level provided by locks, you could install security grilles, gates or shutters. These are particularly useful for protecting basements, where burglars can often work unseen from the street. They can also help provide peace of mind if you have already suffered a burglary, live in a remote area, leave your property unoccupied for long periods of time, or have particularly

valuable possessions, such as works of art or antiques. When buying this type of fitting, look for products that conform to LPS 1175 SR1 or SR2 (*see Chap 3*). A list of suppliers who manufacture products to the standards approved by the police is available on the Secured by Design website (*see Useful Contacts, p 103*).

EXTERNAL SECURITY GRILLES

These are often seen protecting basement windows and some ground-floor windows that open on to quiet back streets. The grille usually comprises an outer steel frame with a number of vertical bars (burglar bars) welded to it, or the bars may be arranged into a pattern of some sort. The grille may be fitted inside the window reveal or to the face of the wall surrounding the window, using frame fixers rather than screws. Most are permanent fixtures and should not be installed over windows that could be needed as emergency exits. Fixed grilles also make it difficult to clean and decorate windows. To meet this need, hinged varieties are available, which are normally secured with a pair of padlocks or integral locks. Grilles installed over outward opening casement windows tend to have the appearance of a cage, allowing the windows to open fully. They can be supplied bare or in a variety of paint finishes, primed or galvanised.

External security grilles have to be

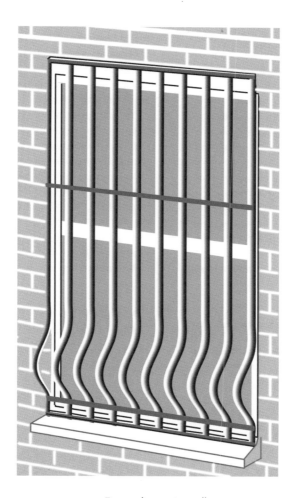

External security grilles

made to measure and are obtainable from most locksmiths, who in turn may source them from a specialist manufacturer. Although it is relatively easy to measure for and install external grilles yourself, it is better to let a locksmith or manufacturer determine the size, and you can carry out the installation if you want. This will ensure that the fixing points are correctly located in the frame and accurately aligned with the brickwork. If there's a mistake in the dimensions, it will be theirs, not yours. Grilles should be secured to the bricks or blocks, not the mortar joints, in accordance with the manufacturer's guidelines.

INTERNAL SECURITY GRILLES

An internal security grille can be hinged, fixed or removable, depending on the application, and must be made to measure. These grilles come in a wide variety of designs, although the most common are diamond and square patterns. Normally, they are supplied with a white powder coated finish, but other colours are available.

Fixed grilles should not be fitted to windows that might be needed as emergency exits. They are attached to the perimeter frame of the window, using the largest screws practical for the frame. Small gaps are incorporated so that you can operate the window handle and stay bar.

Fixed grilles

Fixed grilles can be fitted over glass panels in communal entrance doors (to prevent a burglar from reaching the operating knob on a lock) and on French doors. They can also be used behind traditional leaded lights, although care

is needed to produce an accurate match to the lead pattern. The latter application may not be cost effective for a large number of leaded lights, in which case, collapsible gates would probably be a more sensible solution.

Hinged grilles allow window cleaning, but are still considered permanent fixtures in terms of emergency exits. They are secured in the same manner as fixed grilles and are locked closed with a pair of padlocks or integral locks. One type of removable grille comprises a fixed frame that fits to the window's perimeter frame and a grille section that locates on to four lugs projecting from the fixed frame. One or two of the lugs act as staples for padlocks.

COLLAPSIBLE GATES

Collapsible gates are also known as concertina gates, sliding concertina barriers, and retractable grilles or gates. They are similar to the sliding gates that used to be seen on old-fashioned lifts.

The collapsible gate is widely employed in commercial properties to secure windows and doors, and to close off recessed entrances. Domestic versions, which are made to measure, are nearly always fitted to the inside of doors and windows, sliding along tracks fitted above and below the opening. When open, a gate will only occupy around 15 per cent of the width of a window or door reveal and can be hidden behind a curtain. The gate is secured into a fixed locking stile or, in the case a large opening with two gates, into each other. Most are locked with a key, but you can buy systems that have a 'slam to lock' facility and only require a key for unlocking.

Collapsible gates

SECURITY SHUTTERS

At one time, security shutters were only ever seen on shops and other commercial premises, being used to protect large display windows and add further protection to external doors. They are very effective at keeping burglars at bay, but at some cost to the built environment. They certainly attract graffiti when used in some high-street locations, and many local authorities have introduced planning policies to prevent their use in certain areas. Because of this, if you are considering installing domestic roller shutters, you should approach your local planning department first to see if you need planning permission.

A roller shutter operates in the same manner as a roller blind, except that the horizontal slats run in tracks on each side

Electrically operated shutters

of the window or door opening. They are manufactured from corrosion-resistant aluminium, and come in a wide range of colours and finishes. When open, the shutter is rolled up tightly in a box attached to the brickwork above the opening or at the top of the reveal. A shutter may be opened and closed from indoors with a belt, a crank or an electric motor; remote operation, from inside or out, may also be possible by means of a small radio transmitter. As the shutter closes, it locks automatically. With properties that have an internal door from the garage into the house, the householder can drive up to the garage, operate the roller shutter garage door remotely, drive in and close the door, all without getting out of the car.

Such systems are expensive and usually only installed into homes where there is a very high risk of burglary. Because of the actual, or perceived, high level of risk associated with the use of this product, it would also be very sensible to install an automatic signalling intruder alarm system (*see Chap 7*).

Glass

Any type of glass can be considered a useful barrier against the burglar, because whenever it is broken, the offender risks leaving evidence behind him. Clothing fibres, blood, sweat and fingerprints are the obvious clues to be looked for, but small pieces of glass can also get into the clothing of the person who broke it and anyone standing nearby, and forensic scientists have techniques that enable them to match glass fragments to the scene of a crime. So by fitting good window and door locks, you can force

How to apply safety film to windows

TOOLS AND MATERIALS

- Enough plastic film to cover the windows you want to protect
- Lint-free soft cloth to clean the glass
- Pencil and measuring rule
- Scissors and craft knife
- Hair dryer
- Screwdriver to fit the screws on your window battens

Plastic window film is great for heat insulation and for cutting down on condensation, but better still, it makes it more difficult for the burglar to gain entry, and contains and controls the shards of glass if the window breaks.

1 CUTTING THE FILM

Having removed the existing battens from the inside of the window (or cut new battens to fit), thoroughly clean the glass with the cloth. Use the scissors and craft knife to cut the film so that it covers the glass and so that there is a generous all round fit.

2 SMOOTHING AND EASING THE FILM

Use your hands and the cloth to gently ease the plastic film into place over the surface of the glass. Smooth the film from the centre outwards to remove all air bubbles and wrinkles.

3 SHRINKING THE FILM

With the hairdryer set on a medium heat, gently play it backwards and forwards over the film until it begins to shrink and tighten up on the glass. Continue until the film is indistinguishable from the glass. BE WARNED – go easy, as too much concentrated heat or too much pressure can damage the film and/or break the glass.

4 REPLACING THE BATTENS

Trim away the excess edges from the film with the craft knife, and screw the battens back in place. Be careful not to apply too much pressure to the glass and not to scratch the film.

101

a determined burglar to break glass, and in doing so, you can increase the likelihood that he will be caught. In other words, crime prevention techniques directly assist detection, a factor that sometimes is not appreciated even by the professionals.

Another advantage of some types of glass is the familiar noise it makes when broken, a noise that attracts the attention of people when heard late at night. Another advantage that may not be quite as obvious is that glass contributes towards the powerful crime deterrent of 'natural surveillance'. Because of great advances in glass technology, architects now are able to design buildings with glass walls, and you can often look right through a building and out the other side. This severely hampers burglars, since there are few places to hide.

A variety of glass types are used in the home; all have good and bad points in security terms.

ORDINARY SHEET GLASS

Although this glass can be used in windows, the manufacturing process sometimes causes distortion, so it tends to be used for greenhouses and sheds. It can be cut to any size with an ordinary glass-cutter.

Security value

This type of glass breaks noisily into dangerous shards, and therefore could cause injury to an intruder. However, it's easy to break and has little security value as a barrier.

FLOAT GLASS

This is a distortion-free glass, which is sometimes called plate glass. It is made by floating molten glass on to molten tin. It's commonly used in domestic windows and also in some shop windows. Gradually, however, the float glass in shop windows is being replaced by laminated or toughened glass.

Security value

This glass breaks noisily into dangerous shards, and therefore it could cause injury to an intruder. However, it's easy to break and has little security value as a barrier.

TOUGHENED GLASS

This is used as a safety glass (BS 6206) in a wide variety of applications, including all-glazed doors, glass walls and wherever there is low-level glass in buildings. It is made to measure from specially treated float glass and can't be cut with a glass-cutter.

Security value

Toughened glass breaks relatively quietly into tiny fragments. It can withstand a soft body impact, but it only has to be nicked with a sharp tool to shatter. Because it breaks into such small pieces, it is less able to capture forensic evidence. It has low security properties.

LAMINATED GLASS

This is made from two or more sheets of glass (normally float) or plastic, sandwiched together with one or more inner layers of polyvinyl butyral (PVB). It is used as a security and safety glass, and sometimes as a fire break.

Security value

Laminated glass will break fairly quietly, but will be held together by the tough

PVB inner layer. Consequently, it presents less danger to an intruder than float or sheet glass. The thicker laminates (7.5 mm and above) are used as security barriers, but even the safety laminates of 6.4 and 6.8 mm thickness resist easy penetration and will delay entry. If the glass is simply cracked, it can be left in place until a new piece has been cut to fit.

WIRED GLASS

Normally made from float glass, this glass contains a thin wire mesh that is intended to hold it together if it is broken. It is often used in fire doors and as roofing glass in commercial premises. Most types are not regarded as either a safety glass or security glass.

Security value

Wired glass breaks more easily than laminated glass and does present a danger of injury to an intruder. It resists intrusion, but not to the same extent as laminated glass.

Applied safety and security film

If you want to improve safety, instead of replacing sheet glass with toughened, or toughened glass with laminated, you can apply a film to the inside of a glass pane (*see* DIY project on p 101). Some films reduce UV light damage (which may fade furniture and carpets in a conservatory), while others help keep a conservatory cooler in the summer. Some suppliers will apply the film for you, while others provide DIY kits. For the best results, the film should be applied to the entire sheet of glass. This will require the removal of the glazing beads which are refitted after the film has been applied.

USEFUL CONTACTS

Banham Security
www.banham.com

Chubb Locks
www.chubblocks.co.uk

Cool 4 Summer
www.cool4summer.co.uk

ERA Security
www.era-security.com

Glass and Glazing Federation
www.ggf.co.uk
or search UK sites for 'security film glass'.

Ingersoll Security
www.ingersolllocks.co.uk

Quality Window Films
www.qualitywindowfilms.co.uk

Secured by Design
www.securedbydesign.com

Window Film Directory (The)
www.windowfilmdirectory.co.uk

CHAPTER 5

Garden security and property marking

Garden security

Thirty years ago, thefts from gardens were quite rare, mainly being limited to pranksters swapping neighbours' gates around or transferring a collection of gnomes from one garden to another. There was the odd overnight theft of freshly laid turf or a newly planted shrub, or a bicycle left out, but on the whole gardens, particularly back gardens, were safe from thieves. Even garden tools seemed untouchable, probably because it was too difficult to find a ready buyer for a 15-year-old rake or a rusty lawnmower. To sell on garden plants or tools, the thief needed a market with plenty of potential customers, and there is no doubt that the arrival of the car boot sale in the 1980s contributed to a big rise in garden theft, which has continued to grow steadily since. It is so easy to sell anything to an unsuspecting shopper in the commotion and anonymity of a boot sale. At these events, you will often find somebody selling garden equipment such as old fork handles, spades and seven different lawnmowers. In many cases, these may be the legitimate remnants of several house clearance sales, but someone with 23 planted hanging baskets of different types, all with different plants, has to make you wonder.

During the past two decades, there has been a big rise in the general popularity of gardening and entertaining in the garden. For many, the garden has become an outdoor 'room', with comfortable furniture, cooking facilities and shelter, a place to while away more and more time in the summer. DIY stores and garden centres offer a tempting range of garden accessories, such as dining tables and chairs, heaters and gas barbecues (all designed to be left outside), mature potted trees, and a wide range of statuary and sculptures. Thus, the outlet for stolen property has been matched by a greater availability of property to plunder. Moreover, the fact that many of our homes are better secured may have displaced the risk to the garden instead.

Marking your garden property is one of the most valuable things you can do to safeguard it, because if it is stolen, at least the police will be able to return it to you if it's recovered. It's an unfortunate fact that most of the garden equipment and furniture that comes into the hands of the police cannot be traced to the rightful owners simply because it lacks identification. A lot of this unmarked property is eventually auctioned off, the proceeds going to charity.

Despite this apparently bleak picture, it must be remembered that garden theft is very opportunistic. Often, exercising common sense and taking a few simple precautions will be enough to deter the garden thief. This chapter will help you improve your garden security, but remember that the boundary fences and walls are your first line of defence. Get these right and install an appropriate level of security and aesthetic lighting around the garden (*see Chap 1*).

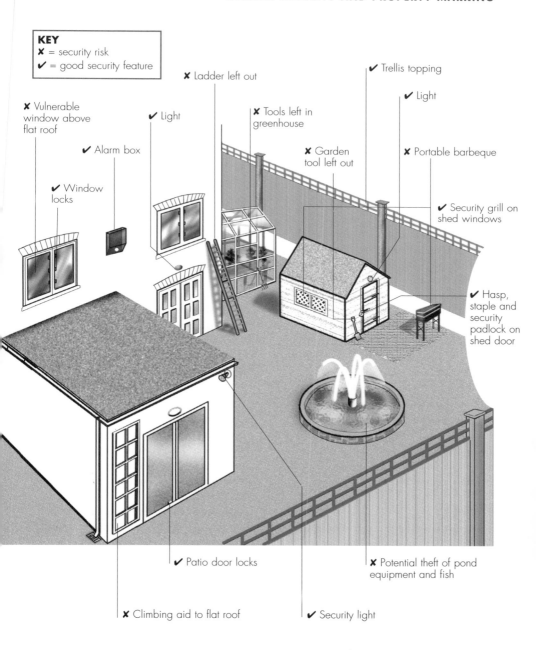

KEY
✘ = security risk
✔ = good security feature

✘ Ladder left out

✔ Trellis topping

✔ Light

✘ Vulnerable window above flat roof

✔ Light

✘ Tools left in greenhouse

✘ Garden tool left out

✘ Portable barbeque

✔ Alarm box

✔ Window locks

✔ Security grill on shed windows

✔ Hasp, staple and security padlock on shed door

✔ Patio door locks

✘ Potential theft of pond equipment and fish

✘ Climbing aid to flat roof

✔ Security light

Security in the garden

Garden buildings

Many gardens contain a variety of buildings, including sheds, garages, greenhouses and conservatories. Each is likely to contain items worth stealing and, just as importantly, tools that can be used to break into your home. Surprisingly, many are quite insecure, given the potential value of some of the contents. Doors often are left unlocked or have no locks, and some garden buildings even have no doors at all.

The first thing to do is make sure that all tools and any expensive items (such as a gas barbecue) are locked away in your most secure outbuilding; invariably, this will be a brick or block built garage. If you don't have a garage, it will have to be the shed; if you only have the tiniest of gardens and have no room for a shed, you should at least buy a tool store (preferably a steel version). A temporary structure like a shed can't be expected to be as secure as your house or garage, but it is still important to take whatever steps are necessary to hinder the progress of a thief. Remember that the leverage and cutting edge provided by a garden spade make it an ideal tool for forcing open a window, even if it is fitted with locks.

SHEDS

Garden sheds range enormously in size, from the small tool store right up to the large summerhouse. Although their construction is generally weak, you can do a lot to deter the thief, or at least slow him down.

Doors Fit at least one BS EN 12320 padlock and fitting at the centre of the door (*see 'Padlocks', p 112*), using coach bolts to secure the hasp and staple or

Typical open shackle padlock

padbar, rather than screws. Adding large washers beneath the bolt heads will help prevent the bolts from pulling through the door if it is forced. If possible, install a steel back-plate on the inside of the door to receive the bolts for maximum strength. Shed doors invariably open outwards, which means that their hinges are exposed. Attach the hinges with coach bolts and make sure that they don't have pins that can be driven out. If they do, you should replace them. At the very least, use clutch-head (non-return) screws to secure the hinges, or cross-head screws with their centres drilled out so that they cannot be unscrewed.

Windows If you never open the shed windows, screw them into their frames – from the inside, if possible. If you can only screw them down from the outside, use cross-head screws and drill out their centres. If you need the windows to open, fit appropriate locks (*see Chap 4*). If you're happy to spend more than a few pounds on your garden security, have security grilles installed on the inside of the windows, or fit flat steel bars.

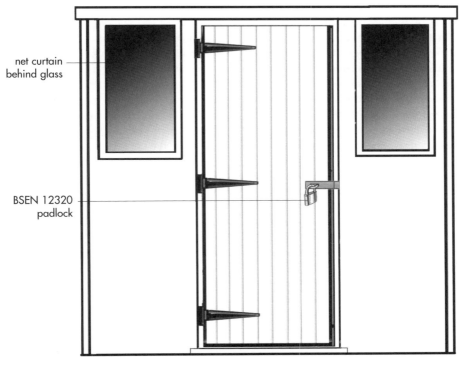

net curtain
behind glass

BSEN 12320
padlock

Shed security

Remember to use coach bolts and washers to attach these items.

Fit the thickest glass possible when replacing broken panes, although the rebate depth in a timber shed is likely to be minimal. Some people use 6.4-mm laminated glass, but the level of extra security this provides will depend on how well you can secure it into the frame. Hanging net curtains or ordinary curtains behind the glass will make it difficult for a burglar to see what you keep in the shed. You could also use reflective plastic film.

Internal security You can buy steel security boxes and cages from most large DIY stores, which can be fixed to the floor joists of the shed, the concrete base or the walls using long screws or expandable bolts. These are ideal for storing valuable items, such as power tools, or dangerous chemicals. You can, of course, make your own wooden box and secure it in the same manner, locking it with a strong hasp, staple and padlock. Don't forget, the object is to slow the thief down as much as possible; if he's managed to get into your secured shed, he's already made some noise and is risking discovery.

To make it more difficult to steal garden spades and forks, you can pass a heavy chain through the handles and attach it to an anchor plate with a padlock. If you keep bicycles inside the shed, chain them to an anchor plate, preferably with an insurance rated D-lock.

Alarm There are plenty of stand-alone outbuilding alarms to choose from. Most are battery powered or work off the mains using an AC adaptor. Nearly all of them employ a passive infra-red detector to sense movement. If triggered, they operate a deafening sounder, making it unpleasant to be in the vicinity. With a little luck, this would warn a trusted neighbour that something's amiss, which is why you should always let your neighbour know when you're going on holiday or away for the weekend.

GREENHOUSES

Obviously, greenhouses are not secure buildings, and nothing of any value should ever be left in one, particularly garden tools. Some greenhouses have a staple on the door and frame, through which you can pass the shackle of a small padlock. The security value of this is limited, but still use it, because if you do unwittingly leave your brand-new stainless steel spade inside, a burglar will have to smash the glass to get to it, risking noise and discovery.

If you cultivate rare or valuable plants in your greenhouse and want to improve their security, without losing the benefits that such a building offers, you could install security cages made from sheets of welded mesh. These can be secured to the ground using plant anchors, or bolted to the building's concrete plinth.

CONSERVATORIES

These very popular structures can add some security to your home, simply because they add an extra skin to the building. But this will only be the case if you continue to lock the original doors and windows of the house as if the conservatory were not there. The security of the conservatory itself will depend upon how it's built, the type of glass used, and the locking arrangements for the doors and any opening windows. If the security of the conservatory is poor and a burglar manages to get inside, any noise he might make breaking into the house would be muffled, and he could also be out of sight of the neighbours.

It is unwise to leave anything of great value in a conservatory because it has vast expanses of glass, which is most likely to be toughened safety glass with all the security weaknesses this brings (*see Chap 4*). However, as with any outbuilding, you can make improvements.

Doors The security of a conservatory door can be improved as described in Chap 3. To prevent collisions with all-glazed doors, place self-adhesive plastic strips on the glass at eye level (for adults and children), or use the plastic peel-and-stick transfers you find in children's books.

Windows If your conservatory has windows that you never open, you can screw them to their frames. It would be sensible, however, to have at least one opening window secured with locks, which is big enough to escape through in an emergency. In most cases, you'll probably want to keep most of the windows as openers to regulate the heat in the building. See Chap 4 for information on appropriate locks.

If your conservatory has automatic opening roof vents that are big enough for a burglar to lever off and climb through, you should consider fixing internal grilles over them.

Replacing the existing toughened glass with laminated glass will be expensive, particularly if the windows are double-glazed. A cheaper option is to apply safety or security film to the inside of the glass, which will help hold it together if it is broken (*see p 101*).

NEW CONSERVATORIES

If you're planning to have a conservatory built, see Chaps 3 and 4 for information on high-security doors and windows, and types of glass. Whether or not you can incorporate enhanced-security doors and windows will depend on how the conservatory is constructed. At the very least, they should have multi-point locking systems. Moreover, any original doors or windows in the external wall of the house should be retained. If you want to create a totally open walk-through into the conservatory, you should consider installing a BS 4737 intruder alarm or extend an existing alarm system to cover the conservatory. You will need BS 6206 safety glass for the doors and windows, but make sure it's either 6.4- or 6.8-mm laminated safety glass rather than toughened, which has no security value.

GARAGES

Detached garages tend to be the most secure outbuildings, as they are usually constructed of bricks, blocks or concrete panels. If the doors and windows are properly secured, a garage should keep 'outdoor' property – including the car – reasonably safe from burglars. The majority of detached garages have a large

main door for the car, a side access door and one or more windows. In effect, they are like a little house and should be secured in the same way. Garages that are integral to the house, or are attached to it, can be secured in the same fashion, but it is particularly important to protect the internal door to the house if there is one. (*see pp 64–5*).

Up-and-over doors This type of garage door has a central locking handle, which is attached by cable or rod to a spring loaded live bolt that engages into a keep in the top of the door frame (some have two live bolts that shoot into the side frames). When the handle is unlocked, it can be turned to release the bolt. If you look at the face of the cylinder lock in the handle, you will often find a number; this refers to the key! Although the cylinder in this type of locking handle can be upgraded by a locksmith, it would be better simply to supplement the lock with additional locks. Another weakness with some single-point locks is that a thin blade can be inserted over the top of the door to slip the bolt. Don't forget that if there is a connecting door into the house, an insecure garage door may provide the perfect opportunity for a burglar.

The first step in securing an up-and-over door is to use the side door as your main entrance. This will enable you to lock the up-and-over door from the inside in a variety of ways. The simplest method is to drill a hole through one of the tracks, just in front of the door's running wheel when it is closed, and place a padlock through it. Sometimes, it is possible to do this on tracks fitted to the side frames. A variety of lockable bolts are available for securing garage doors, either made

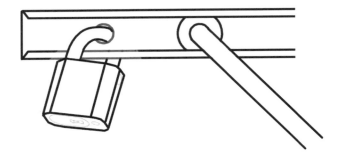

Using a padlock to the running wheel

specifically for the job or that can be adapted. Most will be attached to the door, the bolt shooting into a side frame or the concrete floor slab. Fit them near the bottom of the door.

If there is no side door, or you would prefer to lock the up-and-over door from the outside, the same range of lockable bolts can be used, or you can fit a hasp, staple and padlock. Lockable bolts, padbolts (bolts that accept the shackle of a padlock) and padlocks should be fitted in pairs, one on each side of the door.

Automatic shutters Modern automatic roller shutters will routinely lock when closed and should not require additional locking. However, you should confirm this with the manufacturer (*see pp 99–100*).

Double side-hung doors These are probably best secured with a large hasp and staple, or padbar, and padlock. All fittings should be attached to the door with coach bolts and large washers. Each door should be fitted with a drop bolt to

hold it open safely when driving the car in and out. The second opener should have an additional bolt at the top to secure it to the top of the door frame.

If the doors are 44 mm (1³/4 in) or more thick, they can be locked in a similar fashion to French doors (*see pp 62–3*). In this case, the second opener would be fitted with two lockable bolts, one at the top and one at the bottom (this is particularly important if there are glass panels in the door), and the first opener would have a BS 3621 mortice deadlock or sash lock.

Side doors With a detached garage, the access door can be secured in the same manner as a house back door, although if it is a final-exit door, it should have the same level of security as a front door (*see Chap 3*). A pair of hinge bolts would be useful, particularly if the door opens outwards. An alternative, but effective, way of locking this type of door is to use a mortice sash lock and a mortice deadlock

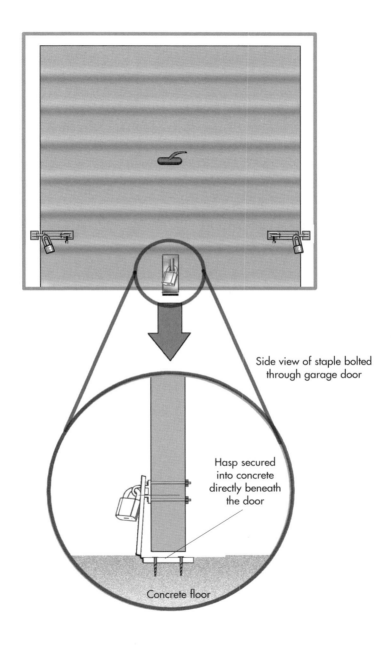

Side view of staple bolted
through garage door

Hasp secured
into concrete
directly beneath
the door

Concrete floor

Examples of how to lock an 'up and over' garage door

(keyed alike), the former being a third of the door's height from the top, and the latter a third of its height from the bottom. See pp 64–5 for methods of securing an internal access door to an integral or attached garage.

Windows These should be secured in the same manner as shed and conservatory windows (*see 'Sheds' and 'Conservatories', pp 106–9*).

Internal security Normally, the garage is the best place to keep long ladders and step-ladders. Hang them on brackets along the walls, locking them in place with chains and padlocks. Additional internal security can be provided in the same manner as for a shed (*see 'Sheds', p 106–8*).

Alarms A house alarm system can be extended to cover a garage, and this is particularly straightforward if the garage is attached to the house. Stand-alone alarms are also suitable (*see 'Sheds', p 106–8*).

PADLOCKS

There are four main types of padlock: open-shackle, long-shackle, closed-shackle and combination. A padlock is used with either a padbar or hasp and staple. Always buy padlocks that conform to BS EN 12320: 2001. The main features you need

Open shackle padlock

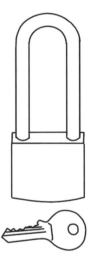

Long shackle padlock

Closed shackle padlock

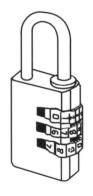

Combination open shackle padlock

to check are corrosion resistance (the padlock and fitting must be suitable for external use) and security rating, which is graded from 1 to 6, where 1 is the lowest and 6 the highest. For most domestic situations, a security grade of 3 or 4 should be sufficient. If in doubt, consult a locksmith. You may also need to check with your insurer that the padlock and fitting are acceptable.

What's at risk in the garden?

LADDERS

Ladders are frequently singled out in crime prevention literature as a number-one useful item for the burglar if left unsecured in the garden. The reality is somewhat different, as ladders are more often stolen than employed in the course of a burglary. In using a ladder, a burglar

risks being seen and heard, and in most cases he will only do this in an isolated location, where it is unlikely there will be any witnesses. Having said that, any ladder or step-ladder should be secured, preferably being locked away in your most secure outbuilding such as your garage or shed. It would be bad enough to come home to find that a burglar had used your ladder against you, but imagine how you'd feel if the ladder had been used to break into your neighbour's house.

If you can't put the ladder in your garage or shed, hang it on brackets fixed to the house wall, a boundary wall or fence. Run a chain or steel cable through the rungs and through a large screw eye fixed securely into the brickwork or a fence post. If you can only store the ladder vertically, keep it away from any

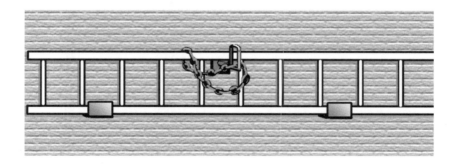

Securing a ladder to a house wall

window and prevent it from being climbed by attaching a 2-m (6 ft 6-in) plank to the rungs with large hooks, passing the cable or chain through holes drilled in the plank.

OTHER CLIMBING AIDS

Consider carefully the potential for climbing from your garden on to flat roofs, up to vulnerable windows, over the fence into your neighbour's garden, or into and out of a back alley or open land. Burglars will use garden chairs and tables, dustbins and any built-in features, such as metal rainwater and soil pipes, as climbing aids. In this situation, you need to apply common sense; you would not want to severely prune a beautiful old wisteria, or other climbing plant or tree just for the sake of security. Instead, you may need to upgrade the security of a window that can be reached because of a climbing aid, treating it as if it were on the ground floor. A garden without the vertical interest provided by climbing plants or trees would be boring; you need to be able to recognise the weaknesses and put them right in a sensitive manner.

If you put out a dustbin or wheelie bin for a morning refuse collection, think twice before doing this the night before. It is not unknown for bins to be used as climbing aids to get into back gardens. If the bin is normally emptied after you go to work, try to reach an arrangement with a neighbour to take it in so that a burglar can't use it.

An external pipe can be made more difficult to climb by fitting a spiked collar around it or by painting a section of it with anti-climb 'non-drying' paint, preferably above 2.25 m (7 ft 4 in) to avoid accidental damage. If you do use anti-climb paint around the outside of your house or on fences, you must display signs warning of the hazard. Reapply the paint at the recommended intervals (because it doesn't stay wet forever) and try to avoid doing this during the autumn, as falling leaves may stick to it. Both items should be available from a locksmith, and you may also find anti-climb paint in a DIY store.

REGULARLY STOLEN GARDEN ITEMS

Among the items that are regularly taken from gardens are potted trees (particularly bay, citrus and palms), hanging baskets, newly planted trees and specimen shrubs, newly laid turf, all types of garden furniture, all types of paving and York stone, fish, ornamental plant boxes, wooden barrels, and pond and swimming-pool pumps. Much of this property is stolen from front gardens in the dead of night, using vehicles; it will be sold on to dealers or at car boot sales within days, and sometimes even hours. Plants of all types account for about a quarter of the property stolen from gardens, so it's worth investing a little time and a few pounds in securing them.

STATUARY AND SCULPTURES

Decorative urns, sculptures, water features and garden ornaments frequently go missing from domestic gardens, and sometimes their theft represents a loss of several thousands of pounds to the householder. Don't think that the sheer size and weight of some of these items will stop them from being taken. Often they are stolen to order, and the thief will come with the right equipment and

Lining your pond with a black bin liner will make it seem deeper than it actually is and could deter the thief

vehicle to remove them. This is so much easier if a statue or sculpture is well away from the house.

To gain some advantage over the thief, be careful not to unwittingly advertise the fact that you possess valuable garden statuary in gardening club newsletters or magazine articles. Ultimately, the security measures you decide to implement will be determined by the value of the item to be protected and the amount you are willing to spend. Here are some prevention techniques to consider:

● Where possible, place the item in view of the house or road, so that any attempt to steal it is likely to be seen. You can increase this possibility by lighting it at night; very valuable items can be monitored by a CCTV camera with a recording facility.

● Place the item within a cordon of soft ground or, if appropriate, in the middle of a pond. Using a black liner in the pond will give the impression that the water is deeper than it really is.

115

● Anchor the item by sitting it over a spike protruding from a heavy base and securing it with some form of adhesive or mortar. Take expert advice before doing this, however, to ensure that you don't damage or otherwise devalue your property.

● Hold the item in position using one or more plant anchors (*see 'Trees, shrubs and containers', opposite*).

● Install a wire-free detector that will activate an alarm in the house.

● Permanently mark the item (*see 'Marking your property', pp 126–30*), photograph it from different angles and make a note of any identifying marks, such as areas of damage and chips.

● Some people have become so concerned about losing a rare statue that they have had an exact copy made and display that in the garden.

● Seek further advice from the police and your insurer, and visit the websites listed in the Useful Contacts on p 136 for more information.

HANGING BASKETS

A cheap method of preventing the theft of hanging baskets or, at least, slowing the

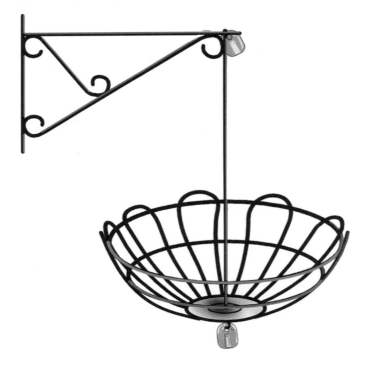

A secure hanging basket

thief down, is to attach the baskets to their brackets with heavy-gauge wire. This is best done by looping the wire in and out of the basket, and then running it up one of the chains to the bracket, where it can be wound around a few times before running back down to the basket. For a little more money, use a plastic coated cable sold for locking cycles. Make sure you buy a long one and simply thread that through the basket, locking it to the bracket.

You can actually obtain lockable hanging baskets through the Internet, and from some garden centres and DIY stores. These incorporate a single, central hanging rod that key locks into a special wall bracket; others have a basket that sits on top of a bracket and is locked in place. Alternatively, you can buy a purpose made clamp that secures the hook of a traditional hanging basket to its bracket.

TREES, SHRUBS AND CONTAINERS

Any trees or shrubs that you have just planted in front of your house are the most vulnerable to theft, because they are clearly new, especially if they still have their labels hanging from them. If the plant is new, its roots would not have developed sufficiently to hold it into the ground. Fortunately, you can secure an expensive new plant with a device called a plant anchor. This comprises a high-tensile steel cable or chain attached to an anchoring device that is driven into the ground and is extremely difficult to remove. The cable or chain can be looped around the base of the tree or shrub, or, come to that, a statue, garden seat or any other vulnerable garden accessory.

A more recent development for

A BASKET CASE

The brief facts in a recent court case described how the accused would drive around residential streets in the summer late at night, unhooking people's hanging baskets from beside their front doors. He would hang them on rails fitted into the roof of his van and would keep going until the rails were full. Then he'd take them to a car boot sale on the following morning and make a handsome profit. His crimes were only discovered when an owner of one of the baskets recognised it at her son's school's car boot sale. She bought it, then summoned the police.

securing container plants is based on a series of corrosion-resistant metal bands. These are secured into the ground through the plant container, using a masonry anchor. The root ball of the plant is placed on top and the metal bands are wrapped around it. The top of each band has a loop through which a plant anchor is threaded and locked in place. This arrangement holds the plant and its container securely to the ground, and it also prevents 'wind rock', which can slow the development of a newly planted tree or shrub, or even kill it.

A cheaper method of deterring the plant thief is to dig a much bigger hole than you would normally need for the root ball and cut a section of chicken wire to the same size. Cut a hole in the wire, small enough to prevent the root ball from pulling through, and pass the upper portion of the plant through it. Then stake out the chicken wire with lengths of wooden batten cut with grooves to hold the wire and pull it firmly into the more

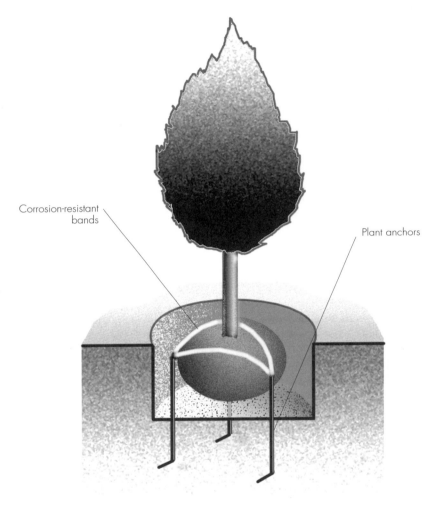

Corrosion-resistant bands

Plant anchors

Securing a specimen tree using plant anchors

compressed subsoil. Finally, back-fill the hole following the planting instructions on the label. Several specimens can be planted in one go using this method; in fact, the more plants there are, the more secure they will be. Don't forget to remove the new plant label, as this will stand out like a sore thumb.

Securing a plant anchor

Secure expensive trees and plants in your garden with this simple but effective device which takes no time at all to intall. This type of anchor is fixed on a concrete surface such as a patio.

TOOLS AND MATERIALS

- Electric drill
- 6-mm drill bit
- Container large enough to fit the plant
- Plant anchor assembly
- Gravel and pebbles
- Chosen potted plant or tree

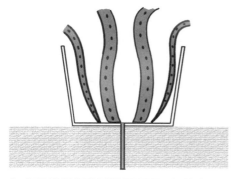

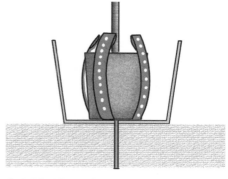

1 ARRANGING THE PLANT ANCHOR

Chose a suitable site and drill a hole into the ground using the 6 mm drill bit. Place the central drainage hole of the container directly over the hole. Arrange the plant anchor assembly in the container and secure it to the ground using the masonry anchor.

2 POSITIONING THE PLANT

Having placed gravel in the base of the plant pot to aid drainage, place your chosen potted plant or tree into the container. Adjust the length of the plant anchor strips so that they fit around the rim of the pot.

3 ENGAGING THE LOCK

Engage the locking mechanism to hold the strips tightly together: your plant is now secure. Fill the remainder of the container with soil to complete the planting. You can also apply a layer of gravel or pebbles to cover the top of the soil and the device. This not only looks good, it also helps retain moisture around the plant.

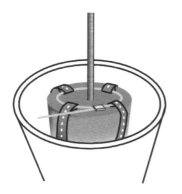

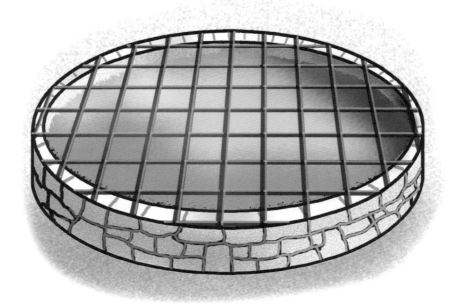

A made-to-measure grille that sits over the pond and locks to a fixed base in several places provides the ultimate security

WATER, POND EQUIPMENT AND FISH

Water can be used as an effective barrier against a burglar, particularly if your garden has a boundary that runs along a canal or river. It can also be used to protect statuary if this is placed in the middle of a deep pond. However, you should never forget that the pond itself might be vulnerable to theft. A statue-based fountain could be at risk, as could any ornament, water pump, lighting, birdbath or fish.

You can protect a submersible pond pump by hiding it well in the pond, making sure the power cables and hoses are buried deeply. If you have the non-submersible type, it should be located in a locked building where it can be securely fixed to the wall. An ornamental fountain with a built-in pump should be fixed to the ground with a plant anchor. Defensive plants in heavy pots can be placed around a pond to make access a little more difficult, provided you are prepared to move them out of the way to maintain the pond.

Some ponds are stocked with fish worth hundreds or even thousands of pounds. Occasionally, they are stolen and, frankly, they are very difficult to protect. Buying time seems to be the best approach, which means a good general standard of security in the garden and boundary fences that can't be climbed easily. A made-to-measure grille that sits over the pond and locks to a fixed base in several places provides the ultimate security. Although, this is an expensive option, it will also prevent children from falling into the pond when your back is turned. Make sure that a grille of this type is strong enough to bear the weight of someone falling on it, and that it sits just above the surface of the water so that fish can come to the surface to catch flies and eat.

Be aware that a water supply can be the source of damage in your garden and home. It is a good idea to have a stopcock inside the house that will turn off the supply to the outside tap. Failing this, use a tap with a detachable handle, or enclose the tap in a locked steel box mounted securely to the house wall.

GARDEN FURNITURE

Store garden furniture in your most secure outbuilding when not in use, but if you can't do this and have to leave it outside, secure it to the ground using plant anchors, chains and padlocks. At the very least, mark the undersides of tables and chairs with your security postcode (*see 'Marking your property', pp 126–30*).

BICYCLES

Although a bicycle is more likely to be stolen when left in the street, precautions should still be taken when it's at home. Children often leave their bikes sprawling outside the front door, and it is difficult to get them to put the machines away safely, but if they're left unsecured in the front garden, they are likely to go missing. Many bicycles are expensive, and an example in

Secure bicycles on a wall bracket to an external wall or to a wall inside a building

121

good condition can fetch a fair bounty for the thief.

The first thing to do is make sure that a bicycle can be locked in the most secure outbuilding you have. For further protection, use a chain, cable or shackle lock, such as a D-lock, to secure it to a wall or floor bracket. If your family has more than one bicycle, chain them all together.

Equally important is to photograph each bike, and record the frame number and any distinctive marks, which will help you identify it should it be taken.

Finally, have the frame engraved or die stamped with your postcode, followed by your house or flat number (*see 'Marking your property', p 126–30*).

For further advice about cycle locks, visit the Sold Secure website operated by the Master Locksmiths Association (*see Useful Contacts, p 136*).

INSURANCE

Very few home insurance policies cover the theft of plants from your garden, but check the extent of your cover with your insurer. Some insurance companies actually sell special policies for gardens, and for a keen gardener who may have spent thousands of pounds on specimen trees and shrubs, and gardening equipment, these are worth investigating.

Vehicles, caravans and boats

Dealing exhaustively with the security of vehicles, caravans and boats goes beyond the scope of this book, but you can find an enormous amount of useful advice by visiting the Home Office websites listed in the Useful Contacts. You can also obtain copies of crime prevention material

specific to vehicles, boats and trailers from your local police station. The information given here relates to vehicles parked in your garage, on your drive or on any hard standing to the front of your house, but not necessarily to on-street parking and car parks.

Vehicles Your car is at its safest when parked in a locked garage. The next safest place is on your drive, behind a gate, especially if a window overlooks the drive, and then on a hard standing in front of your house in full view of the neighbours. A vehicle parked in the street is most at risk. When parking your car away from home, look for a police approved secured car park. This will be indicated by blue 'P' parking signs bearing

When away from home, always try to

the words 'Park Mark safer parking'. You can also search for a town's secured car parks on the Safer Parking Award website (*see Useful Contacts, p 136*).

To protect your car, follow this advice:

- Always lock the doors and close the windows when you park your car, even in a locked garage.

- Never leave anything on display. Thieves will even steal the coins you keep for the car park ticket machine from the ashtray.

- Remove the music system or the detachable fascia when you leave the vehicle.

park your vehicle in a secured car park

- If the car is fitted with an alarm and/or immobiliser, use them.

- Engage the factory fitted steering lock each time you leave the car, or put on your own.

- Tuck in side mirrors and retract telescopic aerials to remove obvious opportunities for vandals.

- Use locking wheel nuts to prevent the wheels from being stolen.

- Have the car registration number or last seven digits of the vehicle identification number (VIN) etched on to the side and back windows, the windscreen and the headlamps.

- Mark any equipment normally left in the car, such as the CD player, the jack and the spare wheel with the car's registration number.

- If the car is very valuable, consider installing a tracking device, which will facilitate its fast recovery.

- Have safety film applied to the side windows to defeat the glass breaking thief (*see p 101*).

Caravans An average of 50 caravans are stolen each week in the UK, many of them from driveways and gardens. Properly locked driveway gates and an appropriate level of security lighting will help deter a thief, but there are a few other things you can also do to minimise the risks.

Since 1992, all caravans manufactured by members of the National Caravan

123

Council have been registered with the Caravan Registration and Identification Scheme (CRIS). The database is accessible to the police and insurance companies to help trace stolen caravans, and to prevent finance and insurance fraud. Since 1997, registered caravans have also been fitted with electronic transponders (tags) so that police can easily check to see if a caravan has been reported stolen. You can register caravans manufactured before 1992 by contacting CRIS (*see Useful Contacts, p 136*). For a small fee and, more importantly, to avoid unwittingly buying a stolen caravan, you can check it out with CRIS (through HPI Check Ltd).

To protect your caravan, follow this advice:

● Keep the door locked, and the windows and any roof lights closed.

● Do not leave items of value on display inside and close the curtains.

● Use locking wheel nuts to prevent the wheels from being stolen.

● Using an indelible-ink pen, write the caravan's vehicle identification number on several areas of bare wood inside, such as under the drawers and on the backs of cupboard doors.

● Fit a cover and hitchlock to the coupling head (towball lock) to prevent the caravan from being towed away.

● Fit a wheel clamp.

● Fit an alarm and add additional security

measures, such as window locks recommended by Sold Secure (*see Useful Contacts, p 136*).

● When storing your caravan, use a secured caravan park (*see Useful Contacts, p 136*).

Motorcycles A motorcycle or moped left in a drive or at the front of a house can be lifted easily on to the back of a truck; it should be secured in much the same way as a bicycle. The following advice will help you reduce the risk of theft substantially:

● Always engage the steering lock and set the alarm if there is one.

● Install a ground anchor, preferably set into concrete, and secure the machine to it with a chain and padlock. Visit the Sold Secure website for tested motorcycle locks.

● Use a motorcycle cover with a locking zip fastener to delay or deter a thief.

● Engrave the vehicle identification number on the machine in more than one place.

● Don't leave anything of value in the panniers or top box.

● You can have an alarm and immobiliser fitted by a professional installer, or add one of a range of DIY systems.

Boats A boat kept on your property or moored on a river or canal at the bottom of your garden is vulnerable to theft, as are the contents. Since 1998, all new boats have been installed with electronic tags, which contain the Hull Identification Number (HIN). Secondhand boats can also be tagged. For more information, visit the websites given in the Useful Contacts. If a boat is stored on your property, take the following steps to reduce risks:

● Immobilise the trailer by fitting a wheel clamp and securing the coupling head (*see 'Caravans', pp 123–4*).

● Remove the outboard motor if practical and store it in a substantial, secured building. Otherwise, bolt it securely in place using lockable nut shrouds.

● Don't leave anything of value on display in or on the boat, particularly if it is not to be used for some time. During storage, remove the radio, life-raft and life jackets if they can be stored in a more substantial building, and keep the boat locked.

● Install an alarm system and display the 'This boat is alarmed' sticker that is normally supplied.

● Check that the cockpit lockers, hatches and main entrances are securely locked. Be prepared to fit additional locking devices.

Motorcycle ground anchor

- Consider installing a steel strong-box for the storage of valuables. This will be particularly useful when the boat is in use.

- Record the serial numbers of any expensive items on the boat, such as a radio and other marine equipment. They should also be marked with the HIN and your security postcode.

- Don't leave boat documents on board when it is unoccupied, and take all keys with you.

Marking your property

The subject of property marking has been included in this chapter because the items in your garden are so vulnerable to theft. Also, it's really easy to mark the things you keep in the garden or outbuildings. Having said that, it is vital to mark items indoors as well.

The Home Office and police have been advising people to mark property with their postcodes for years, but it seems that only about 5 per cent of the population actually do it. Marking property is not just about being able to retrieve it; the technique can help solve crimes and punish offenders. Recovered property, which isn't identifiable, can greatly frustrate the police investigation of a crime. In some cases, the decision to prosecute or the outcome of a trial may hinge solely on the police's ability to link a recovered item of property to the scene of a crime.

A variety of companies offer property marking systems, and operate private property registers and databases. The Loss Prevention Certification Board has

---

TWO FOR THE PRICE OF ONE
A known burglar riding a fairly new bicycle was stopped in the street by the police. When they turned the bike over, they found that the owner's security postcode had been stamped on the bottom of the crank casing – and it was not the postcode of the burglar's home address. They arrested and searched him, finding jewellery and credit cards in his pockets, which he admitted to having stolen from the same house from which he had taken the bicycle. The officers contacted some colleagues by radio, asking them to visit the house to secure it. Imagine their surprise when, upon arrival, they discovered a second burglar, unconnected to the first, climbing out of a side window with a video recorder.

---

set standards for these so that potential users can be sure of a minimum level of performance. In the case of property marking, look for systems that comply with LPS 1225; choose a register or database that complies with LPS 1224 Further information can be obtained from the Loss Prevention Certification Board, BRE, Garston, Hertfordshire, WD25 9XX, or in précis form by visiting www.crimereduction.gov.uk/property01.htm

Marking your property in a permanent manner, and then advertising the fact by displaying a police or commercially produced sticker, can deter a thief from stealing it in the first place. This is because the marks will be difficult to remove and, of course, he'll run the risk of being caught in possession of it. If he's not deterred, he'll have the bother of removing the marks later, because if he doesn't, he may find it difficult to sell the

Engraving the postcode

property. Police do recover property where attempts have been made to remove the marks, but forensic scientists have methods that sometimes enable them to read the original code, so all is not lost.

Apart from jewellery, valuable antiques, works of art and other items that would be damaged by permanent visible marking, it is possible to mark most items in your home. The things you should mark include all electrical goods, leather goods and designer clothes, purses, wallets and handbags, items of furniture, mobile phones and other portable personal property.

Garden items are easy to mark. Outdoor tables and chairs should be marked with indelible ink on the bottom and also have an engraved code. Garden

tools should be engraved in a number of visible places, because the marks will not detract from their value. With equipment such as a lawnmower or electric drill, you can scratch the postcode into their plastic bodies in a number of places.

Don't forget to look for postcodes if you're buying secondhand goods, because if you find one, the item might be stolen – remember, discovering marked property may lead to the solving of a serious crime.

Using postcodes to mark property is a sensible approach, because we are already familiar with them; the combination of a postcode and house number creates a unique code for every address in the country. Police stations have access to all the national postcodes, so it's easy for the police to trace the source of any marked items they recover.

WORKING OUT YOUR SECURITY POSTCODE

The police recommend that you mark your property with your full postcode, followed by your house or flat number, or the first two letters of the name of the house if there is no number. If you move house or sell the marked property, put an 'X' at the end of the code. The new code should be placed nearby.

The following examples will show you how to work out your security postcode:

Street address: 9 Smith Street
Postcode: BX1 4RS.
Security code: BX1 4RS 9

Street address: Flat 5, 22 Smith Street
Postcode: BX1 4RV
Security code: BX1 4RV 22/5

Street address: Fairview, Smith Street
Postcode: BX1 4RS
Security code: BX1 4RS FA

If the householder in the last example changed their address to Bestview, Smithier Street, BX1 5RJ, they would place an X after the original security code (BX1 4RS FA X) and engrave a new code (BX1 5RJ BE) next to it.

MARKING METHODS

Stamped, engraved and chemically-etched visible security codes are difficult to remove and are the police preferred method for marking the property in your home. Hand and electric engraving tools, and chemical etching kits can be bought from hobby shops and some DIY stores (*see Useful Contacts, p 136*). It may be possible to borrow some of these items

from your local Neighbourhood Watch co-ordinator or from the local police crime prevention department. When you have marked the property in your home and garden, display stickers on windows to advertise the fact. Don't be tempted to display 'marked property' stickers if you haven't marked your possessions, as this could devalue the scheme.

In the garden, you may consider marking flowerpots that contain expensive trees or shrubs. Although the thief may repot the plant before attempting to sell it, he may still be caught out if he forgets to dispose of the original pot.

If by engraving or punching a mark, you risk damaging an item, you can use an ultra-violet ink pen instead. Ultra-violet ink is barely visible in normal daylight, but fluoresces under ultra-violet light. It's best applied to porous surfaces, as the ink will soak in and be difficult to remove. Unfortunately, it tends to fade with time and needs to be reapplied every six months or so. This means that you will need a small ultra-violet lamp to check if the mark is still visible. When using ultra-violet ink, try to apply it on under surfaces to prolong its life. However, it should only be used as a last resort.

SECURITY CODING BICYCLES

A bicycle can be marked with a security postcode using die punches. To do this, turn the bicycle over and scrape off a small amount of paint from under the crank casing with a file – just enough to accommodate the code. Hold the die stamp firmly in place and give it a sharp blow with a hammer. One strike should do it, but if two are required due to the hardness of the metal, make sure you hold the die in exactly the same place, otherwise you'll end up with a double mark that may be mistaken for another letter or number. Once you have stamped in the security postcode, paint over it with an outdoor clear varnish. This will prevent rusting of the exposed metal surface and ensure the postcode is visible for inspection. A lot of police stations and cycle dealers can provide 'property marked' stickers to put on your bike. For a small charge, cycle shops will mark your bike for you, and may do it for free if you've just bought the bike from them.

ANTIQUES AND WORKS OF ART
The normal means of security marking property can't be used for antiques and works of art, but there are other products that can be employed, which are unlikely to cause damage. One is a chemical compound that contains ultra-violet-sensitive die and a unique DNA element; another is a micro marking solution containing microdots that carry details of the owner, such as the security postcode or a unique reference number. It is essential that property marked in this way also carries information that will advise

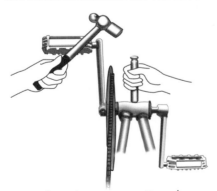

Stamping your security code

the police to search for the marks. Before marking antiques or works of art, contact an expert. For further information about these products, *see the Useful Contacts, p 136.*

TAKING PHOTOGRAPHS
If you don't intend to mark an item, or can't because you have been advised not to, you must write out a description of it and take photographs to aid identification. When photographing a valuable item of property, note the following advice:

● Detail is essential. Use a digital camera on a high pixel setting or colour film of 200 or 400 ISO.

● Get as close to the object as you can while keeping it in focus. You might be able to get closer than the boundaries of the view-finder. This is a lot easier to do if you use a digital camera because you can see the result immediately and take it again if you're not satisfied with the result.

● Place a familiar item next to the object, such as a ruler or stamp, to indicate its size.

● Take photographs of single objects rather than groups, otherwise you risk losing detail.

● Depending on the object you are photographing, take views of the back, front and sides, and if necessary of the top and bottom. You can also photograph a unique part of the item or an area of damage, which would help with its identification.

- Take photographs in natural daylight to reduce the effect of reflected light. Avoid flash photography, especially if the object is made of glass, reflective metal or is highly glazed.

- Photograph objects against non-reflective, plain backgrounds. A dark background is ideal for glass and silver. Use a light background for other items. With a digital camera, you can experiment with different backgrounds until you obtain the best result.

- Store your photographs and negatives separately, with one set away from your home and another in a fire-resistant cabinet if you have one. Copy digital photographs on to two sets of discs and store in a similar fashion.

- Combine your photographs with a written description of each item, and contact your insurer to see if they have any other requirements. Photographs taken for evaluation purposes may not provide sufficient detail.

- A video recording of a specific valuable object may not provide sufficient detail. However, it can be used as a general record of the contents of your house. Photographic and video records of your property are particularly useful if you have to make an insurance claim for theft or damage.

COMPILING DESCRIPTIONS

Fine art A photograph of the picture is essential, but look out for reflected light from glass, which may ruin the detail of the photograph. Record the artist's name and write a description of the scene or subject. Describing a particularly unique part of the picture would be useful. Note whether it is executed in oils, watercolours or some other medium, and describe the material upon which it has been painted. Record the size of the picture and the frame, and any areas of damage or repair. Note down any marks made on the backing board and, if you can, take a photograph of the canvas to highlight the weave pattern.

Furniture Take photographs and record areas of damage. Consult an antiques expert before marking wooden furniture; many people mark the bottoms of drawers, and the undersides of tables and chairs with a security postcode using ultra-violet and indelible-ink pens.

Clocks and watches Take photos in natural light to avoid any reflections. Record the maker's name, model, and the type of numeral and face. Describe the details of the movement if you know them, and note any repairer's marks and areas of damage, indicating their locations.

Silver Take photos in natural light. Note the maker's name or initials together with any other identifiable marks, such as the original owner's initials, hallmarks and engravings.

Jewellery Keep a jeweller's valuation certificate in a safe place together with a photograph. If there is no valuation certificate, consider having a valuation done. Otherwise write down a full description of the item, detailing the type and colour of any metal and stone, its setting and any hallmarks found. If you want to wear valuable items of jewellery to an event, keep them covered up or otherwise secured until you arrive.

Safes

Although marking property and compiling descriptions are very important methods of protecting your property, it makes sense to further secure those items that are commonly stolen in burglaries (cash and jewellery) by storing them in a safe.

Safes come in various sizes, shapes and weights, and provide a good level of protection for cash and other valuable items, such as jewellery, important documents and data. Some people have to install a safe as a condition of their insurance, but it's a good idea for everyone to have one.

The security of a safe is determined by its construction, the strength of its sides and door or lid, the strength and complexity of its locking system, and its fixing. All four elements are equally important, because even the strongest domestic safe can be opened if the burglar can take it away from your home and work on it at his leisure.

A safe may be locked with keys or a combination lock. Some have a key and combination or two combinations, depending on the level of risk and the insurer's requirements. Keep spare keys or a record of the combination in a separate place away from your home, preferably in a safe deposit box at a bank. Bear in mind that an ordinary security safe will not protect its contents in the event of a fire (see 'Fire and data safes', pp 134–5).

STANDARDS AND CASH RATINGS

Safe manufacturers give their products a cash rating, which can start from as low as £750 and go right up to £150,000. This is based on the European industry standard for security testing of safes, which is BS EN 1143-1: 1997. The cash ratings are a good guide to the security offered by a safe: O is the lowest standard and VI the highest (see 'Eurograde' table below). The Loss Prevention Certification Board evaluates safes to this standard, so look for the LPCB certification mark. If you intend buying a secondhand safe, look for one that has been reconditioned in accordance with BS 7582.

If you're thinking of buying a safe, speak to your insurer first to make sure that you obtain the right grade for your risk. The amount of cover your insurer offers on a particular model of safe may be higher or lower than its cash rating, and may also be adjusted depending on whether it has been installed professionally or by yourself. The way in which a safe is installed is just as important as the safe itself. Some insurers will not cover a DIY-installed safe and will insist on it being installed by the manufacturer or their authorised agent, so check first.

Cash ratings are normally multiplied by ten for any items of jewellery you might want to keep in the safe. This means that you could store £60,000 worth of jewellery in a safe with a cash rating of £6,000. If you wanted to keep, say, £2,000 in cash in the same £6,000 cash rated safe, you could only have jewellery to the value of £40,000 with it.

EUROGRADE SAFE CASH RATINGS	
O	up to £6,000
I	up to £10,000
II	up to £17,500
III	up to £35,000
IV	up to £60,000
V	up to £100,000
VI	up to £150,000

TYPES OF SAFE

Wall safe The dimensions of wall safes match multiples of standard brick sizes, commonly two, three or four bricks, and are normally no deeper than 125 mm (5 in). The back-plate of the safe is often larger than the overall body size and sits behind the bricks when the safe has been fixed in place. This is to prevent it from being chipped out of the wall. Some examples also include side lugs and/or fixing holes to further secure the safe into the brickwork once it has been mortared into place. Most wall safes have a maximum cash rating of £1,500, reflecting the inherent weakness of the design, which can be knocked out of a wall. This rarely occurs, however, and a wall safe would suit most domestic situations, where often the need is to secure a few hundred pounds and a little jewellery. It's a good idea to conceal the location of a wall safe by installing it behind a cupboard with an access cut-out in the back, or at the very least behind a picture or a mirror, as they do in the movies.

Under-floor safe The most secure floor safes are set in concrete and normally have cash ratings of £3,000 to £35,000. An existing concrete floor will have to be excavated and damp-proofed before a safe can be fitted, so sometimes the cost of installation can be higher than the cost of the safe, unless you do it yourself. This type of safe can also be set into concrete beneath a suspended floor, but there will

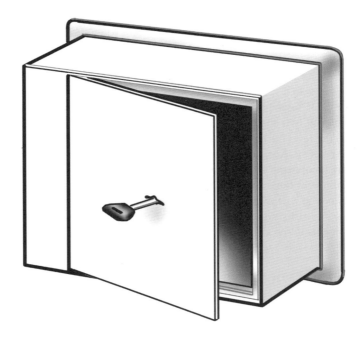

Typical wall safe

How to fit a floor-standing safe

What are you going to do with all those small items of value that you have lying around the house? It a problem! The swift and easy low-cost answer is to fit a floor safe – one that tucks away beneath a wooden floor.

TOOLS AND MATERIALS

- Top quality BS under-floor safe – one that is designed to fit between the joists – with screws to fit
- Short bladed floorboard saw
- Hammer

- Cold bolster chisel or wrecking bar
- Pencil and measuring rule
- Bevel-edged chisel
- Screwdriver to fit the screws
- Sandpaper

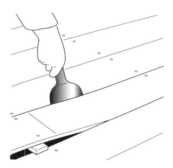

1 SEPARATING THE FLOORBOARDS
Having decided where you want to fit the safe, gently saw through the tongues that link neighbouring floorboards. Be careful not to damage underfloor pipes and cables. **NOTE:** if you have a chipboard floor, you will have to modify the procedures accordingly.

2 REMOVING THE FLOORBOARDS
Use the hammer and the bolster chisel to ease and lever up the boards. Having wedged the board up with a short length of batten, pencil in a guide mark across the board – meaning a mark that is flush with the side of the joists – and cut the board through with the saw.

3 FITTING THE SAFE AND FINISHING
Set your safe in place so that it bridges the joists and try it out for fit. Depending on the size and design of your safe, you may have to add extra supports by screwing short trimmers between existing joists. When you are happy with the fit, take the chisel and cut a rebate for the fitting flange – so that the safe fits flush with the top of the joists. Finally, screw the safe in place, sand and polish all the sawn edges of the boards, and set them in place so that the safe is hidden from view.

Typical under-floor safe

be an added cost for timber shuttering to form the necessary large concrete block.

Some under-floor safes are designed to be secured between a pair of joists and may be referred to as floorboard safes. Although the manufacturer might give this type a cash rating, you should check with your insurer before installing one.

Floor-standing safe These safes have cash ratings from £1,500 to £150,000 and, unlike the safes described previously, can be taken with you when you move house. They must be secured to the floor

(preferably into concrete) and/or wall, as otherwise they can be stolen. Some people install a floor-standing safe in the bottom of a cupboard or under the stairs, as they tend not to be the most attractive items of furniture.

Fire safe This type of safe is designed to protect documents during a fire. It will keep the temperature inside to below the point at which paper ignites for one or two hours, or more, depending on its rating. Some fire safes have a cash rating, but most are not intended to hold computer data, which is destroyed at a much lower temperature than can be achieved in a normal fire safe.

Data safes and computers A data safe is used to protect computer data during a fire and is designed to keep the temperature inside below the point at which data is corrupted or destroyed, which is about 52°C. It can be used to store papers, tapes, discs, CDs, etc. Some data safes have a cash rating, but they are not generally intended for cash storage. In any event, it is sensible to store backed-up data away from your home, either on discs or with an off-site server.

You can buy a range of devices to secure you computer equipment, such as locking cabinets and clamps. These should comply with LPS:1214 test standard by the Loss Prevention Certification Board. If you work from home and use a computer, you should protect your livelihood with the best physical and electronic security you can afford.

Typical floor-standing safe

USEFUL CONTACTS

Artguard
www.artguard.co.uk

British Antique Dealers' Association (The)
www.bada.org

British Marine Industries Federation
www.britishmarine.co.uk

British Parking Association (The)
www.britishparking.co.uk

Caravan Registration and Identification Scheme (CRIS)
(01722 411430)

Crocus
www.crocus.co.uk/whatsgoingon/gardentroubles

Garden Xtras.com
www.gardenxtras.com

Home Office websites
www.secureyourmotor.gov.uk
www.crimereduction.gov.uk

Interior Landscaping Products
www.interiorlandscaping.co.uk/hanging.htm

Leisure and Outdoor Furniture Association
www.lofa.com

Motor Insurance Repair Research Centre, Thatcham (The)
www.thatcham.org

National Caravan Council
www.nationalcaravan.co.uk

Plant Anchor Ltd
www.plantanchor.com

Retail Motor Industry Federation
www.rmif.co.uk

Safer Parking Award (Scheme)
www.securedbydesign.com

Secured Caravan Park
www.securedbydesign.com

Secured by Design
www.securedbydesign.com
Click on 'Licence Holders' then on 'Property Identification' for property marking equipment, computer security and service providers.

Society of Motor Manufacturers and Traders
www.smmt.co.uk

Sold Secure
www.soldsecure.com

Topiary Shop
www.topiaryshop.co.uk

Trace (stolen antiques recovery service and magazine)
www.trace.co.uk

Tracker
www.ncs-systems.com/tracker

Vehicle Systems Installation Board (for fitting car alarms and immobilisers)
www.vsib.co.uk

CHAPTER 6

Security lighting

Lighting around your home at night can be an effective deterrent against an intruder, making it difficult, if not impossible, for him to work unobserved. It is most effective when applied as a part of a package of home security improvements, such as those suggested in this book.

Many people install lighting around their homes not only to deter burglars, but also to give them a sense of security when returning home at night. For example, a light that illuminates a front door provides a welcoming atmosphere, but in addition allows callers to be identified without having to open the door. A light fitted to the back of the house will help you see your way to the garage or dustbins, make it easier to unload the car after dark or light up a summer party in the garden. Moreover, lighting can highlight architectural and landscape features, enhancing the appearance of your home and garden.

This chapter will help you choose the most appropriate type of security lighting for your home. For further information, contact a lighting manufacturer or installer. Some offer a free lighting planning and technical support service (*see Useful Contacts, p 149*). Your local police crime reduction officer may also be able to provide details of specialist lighting companies.

Choosing security lighting

A wide variety of security lighting is available. Light units come in a range of sizes to cater for all types of installation. There are lights with sensors, some with high-wattage lamps, others with energy-efficient lamps, lanterns that fit on a wall, and others that fix into the ground, such as spiked lights or post mounted globes.

Choosing the right type can be difficult. You may base your decision purely on a particular style or shape of lantern, but you must make sure that it will provide the appropriate amount of light for its location. Alternatively, you may be more concerned about the running cost of the lamps. As a general rule, lamp and luminaire (light fitting) combinations that are inexpensive are more costly to run. There are specific advantages and disadvantages with all lamp types, as well as issues of suitability with certain types of luminaire.

LUMINAIRES

A luminaire is a complete electric light fitting, the purpose of which is to direct, filter and distribute the light to where it is needed. It will contain the control equipment and possibly a detector or timer, as well as all the parts that are necessary to support and protect the lamp. It does not include the lamp itself.

The majority of outdoor light fittings have protective weather sealed casings, made of a robust material that should resist attack by a burglar. As a rule, polycarbonate light fittings offer the best resistance, but if glass is used, the fittings must be positioned out of reach. Ideally, light fittings should be mounted to walls around the outside of the property or to outbuildings, and many people prefer the bulkhead type of fitting for this purpose. These are ideal for small properties or to light areas such as narrow pathways.

For a large garden and front driveway, consider using illuminated bollards to mark pathways and entrances. Alternatively, you could install lighting on tall posts to increase the spread of light. In this instance, seek expert advice before deciding on the type of lighting.

LIGHT POLLUTION

Outdoor lighting can have a detrimental effect on the local environment. When installing lights, you must consider light pollution, and use a luminaire that directs the light downwards and horizontally, rather than upwards. You must strike a balance between the need to increase the security of your property and the possible side-effects that the light may have on your neighbours and local wildlife. Badly positioned fittings can direct light into neighbours' homes and gardens, and can cause great annoyance, often leading to disputes. Preventing uncontrolled glare is equally important, as it can dazzle motorists and pedestrians. Vertical light spill from non-directional fittings, such as globes and some other decorative luminaires, not only wastes light, but also is particularly annoying to astronomers.

In an ideal world, outdoor security lighting, particularly at the side and rear of a house, would only come on when it recognised a criminal tip-toeing across the lawn. Unfortunately, this type of lighting does not exist, even if a number of 'off-the-shelf' products suggest otherwise.

Lamps

The right choice of lamp can make a significant difference to the security of your home. When choosing a lamp there are three key features to consider:

- **Efficacy** This is the technical term to describe the efficiency of a lamp at converting electricity into visible light. The amount of light produced is expressed as the number of lumens emitted for each watt of energy input. The best lamp at generating light is the monochromatic (orange), low-pressure sodium lamp, which is commonly used in many street lights. Some of these can generate about 200 lumens per watt, compared to around ten lumens for a standard domestic tungsten-filament light bulb.

- **Colour** A key aspect of good lighting is colour rendering, which is the ability of a lamp's light to make colours identifiable. Colour is important, as the human eye has evolved to use sunlight, which contains the full colour spectrum. Colour appearance is often expressed by such terms as 'cool', 'intermediate' and 'warm'. This is particularly relevant if you want a security light to enhance the appearance of a building. For security lighting to be effective, you need to choose a light source that provides good colour rendering.

- **Controllability** It is essential to control where the spread of light falls. In general, the smaller the light emitting part of the lamp (the arc tube), the easier it is to control. This can be demonstrated by comparing the two most popular types of security light fitting: the floodlight and the spotlight. Both provide powerful illumination, but the spread of light is fundamentally different. A floodlight generates a wide spread of light that gradually declines

Bulkhead light

at the edges, whereas the spotlight directs a concentrated beam of light with sharp edges at a fixed point. The correct positioning of fittings is essential to ensure that the light is aimed where it is required. For example, a front entrance light should be placed so that callers can be seen and are well lit, while the occupier can stay back out of the light. A poorly positioned light could leave the caller in shadow, which would detract from the purpose of fitting it. This consideration is equally important when siting additional lamps around the property, where pools of light may inadvertently create areas of shadow in which an intruder could hide.

The front of the house is well illuminated and allows callers to be lit as they approach the house

Tungsten-halogen flood lamp

TUNGSTEN LIGHT BULB

The ordinary domestic tungsten light bulb is a filament lamp. It has an average lifespan of about 1,000 hours. Since the UK has over 3,900 hours of darkness annually, it is likely that this type of lamp will need replacing at least four times a year if it is used outdoors on a timer or solar switch. However, these bulbs are inexpensive and produce instant light as soon as they are switched on. They also give very good colour rendering, but they're not very efficient, producing only 11 lumens of light for each watt consumed.

TUNGSTEN-HALOGEN LAMP

The tungsten-halogen lamp is commonly used for floodlighting and probably generates the most complaints about light pollution – as a result of badly positioned luminaires. These lamps have an average life of 2,000 hours. They range from the domestic sizes of 150 to 500 watts, but can be rated as high as 2,000 watts for

Photoelectric cell operated security lighting allows callers to be clearly visible

commercial or industrial lighting schemes. They produce about 20 lumens of light per watt and give instant light, but, as the wattage suggests, they consume more electricity to work. This type of lamp is often sold in DIY stores as an external security light, complete with a waterproof luminaire and a passive infra-red detector that switches the lamp on when triggered. Invariably, they are installed on the back walls of houses and will illuminate the length of an average back garden.

COMPACT FLUORESCENT LAMP

The compact fluorescent lamp produces around 40 lumens per watt, so it is a great deal more efficient than a filament lamp. It requires special control gear between the lamp and the mains electricity supply. You can buy this type of lamp as part of a complete light unit, but more commonly it's bought as a replacement lamp for a tungsten light bulb. Local authorities are keen to encourage the more efficient use of energy, and an easy way to do this is to swap your ordinary light bulbs for compact fluorescent lamps. Although they are a lot more expensive than ordinary light bulbs, they last much longer (typically 5,000 hours) and use a lot less electricity. Consequently, they work out considerably cheaper in the long run. When you switch the lamp on, it produces instant light, but needs to warm up for about a minute to reach its maximum output.

TUBULAR FLUORESCENT LAMP

This is a general-purpose lamp for short-range use, and it is more commonly employed indoors than outside. It produces immediate white light; in very cold weather, however, the light output can be significantly reduced outdoors.

HIGH-PRESSURE SODIUM LAMP

This lamp gives about 90 lumens of light per watt and produces a pinkish-white light, as compared to the orange glow of a low-pressure sodium lamp. The wattage range is between 50 and 1,000 watts. Its lifespan is in excess of 8,000 hours, which makes it very economic to run. This type of lamp requires a 'strike time' of between one and five minutes, which is the time required for the lamp to warm up before reaching its maximum output. High-pressure sodium lamps are used mainly to illuminate streets, but they can also be found along driveways and in car parks; sometimes they are used to illuminate wide frontages of large houses. The lamp's colour rendition is not as good as the lamps described previously. In a domestic situation, the high-pressure sodium lamp is best used to illuminate the grounds of large houses, where background light is required for long periods during the night.

LOW-WATTAGE LAMPS

There is a wide range of low-wattage garden lights to choose from, including solar powered examples. They are available from DIY stores and garden centres, and are more suitable for creating lighting effects than for security. Most are designed to sit in flower borders, act as uplighters for trees and shrubs, or mark the edges of a driveway or path. They have a tendency to create dark shadows. For security, these lights should be supplemented with the brighter types already described.

Switching

The full benefit of security lighting will only be realised if the lights can be turned on automatically at the right time. You can do this in several ways.

PHOTOELECTRIC CELL

A photoelectric cell will switch on a lamp when the amount of light detected by the cell falls below a predetermined level; it will turn off the lamp when the amount of light rises above the preset level. A photoelectric cell normally incorporates a time delay to prevent the lamp from being turned on by a sudden drop in light level caused by fast moving, dark rain clouds or by passing car headlights. In other words, the cell will only switch on the light when it's needed. Photoelectric cells are very reliable and require little maintenance, other then a periodic wipe with a damp cloth. For more precise control, you can buy outdoor light fittings that incorporate both a photoelectric cell and a timer. That way, you can ensure that the light can only be turned on at certain times of the day.

PASSIVE INFRA-RED DETECTOR

A passive infra-red detector (PIR) operates by sensing the movement and change in level of infra-red energy within its field of view. It doesn't 'look' at the entire area within its range, but detects infra-red energy from a pattern of smaller zones. This means that the detector is more sensitive to movement across its field of view than towards it. Security lights bought at DIY stores usually combine this type of detector with a spotlight or floodlight containing a tungsten-halogen lamp. Most people install the light fitting on the back wall of the house and aim it down the garden.

One of the problems with this arrangement is that the detector can't tell the difference between a neighbour's cat and a burglar. Consequently, the powerful light could be switched on and off needlessly on many occasions, which could reduce the life of the lamp. Nevertheless, the combination is very useful, and by adjusting the angle of the PIR, you can reduce the rate of 'false' switching. If you tilt the PIR downwards, only close approaches to the house will be detected; alternatively, reducing the angle will mean that the detector looks over the heads of any local cats. However, if you set the angle too high, you could pick up cats walking along the top of the back fence. Some PIRs have quite a wide angle of view, making it possible for your neighbour to switch the light on from their garden. It's a matter of finding a suitable compromise. Some models allow you to adjust the sensitivity of the PIR.

TIMED AND MANUAL SWITCHING

Time switches simply turn the lights on and off at the times you set. They must be reset periodically to stay in line with seasonal changes. A disadvantage of a time switch is that a power cut could make it lose its time setting, requiring it to be reprogrammed. It is possible to buy a time switch fitted with a solar dial that incorporates either an electronically wound clockwork motor or an electronic motor with a spring reserve. This allows the unit to run for a number of hours without electrical power.

Some people may prefer simply to switch on the lights manually when it gets dark. This works well provided there is always someone at home to do so. A house in total darkness during late afternoon in the winter makes an obvious statement that no one is at home.

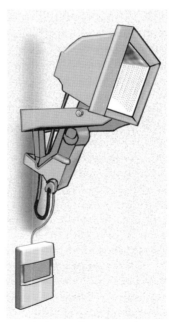

Tungsten-halogen flood lamp fitted with a passive infrared detector (PIR)

143

An alternative is to have a combination of automatically switched lamps with one or two that are manually switched. For example, a tungsten-halogen lamp fitted to the back wall of a house could have its switch in an upstairs bedroom. This would allow the back garden to be observed from a vantage point behind the bright light source, which hides the observer. In this way, you would have total control over the light, only switching it on if needed to do so.

INDOOR TIME SWITCHES

To complement outdoor security lighting, don't forget the security lighting inside your home. A wide variety of indoor time switches are available from DIY stores, including some that plug into a wall socket or a standard ceiling light fitting; others can be fitted in place of a wall light switch. Most cater for 24-hour programming for up to seven days with random on/off switching. Some incorporate a battery back-up in case of power failure. Alternatively, you can buy battery operated sensor lights that function in a similar way. When using these switches, it is important to distribute them around your home so that the lights are turned on and off in a manner that reflects your normal domestic routine.

For most people, this means turning lights on in the lounge, dining-room and kitchen from when it gets dark until bedtime, with additional timed lights coming on in the bedrooms and perhaps the bathroom later in the evening. It's a good idea to have lights showing to the back and front of your home. It's essential to make your home look occupied. Lights left on only in the hallway and on the landing at, say, 10pm might actually suggest that nobody is at home.

GOING ON HOLIDAY

If you don't have timers for your lights, ask a trusted neighbour to pop in each evening and turn some on (and off again later). Even if you do have timers, it's important that your neighbour comes in each day to draw the curtains so that when your timed lights come on, you're not showing everyone in the street (including potential burglars) the contents of your home.

Your neighbour will also be able to pick up any post or junk mail that has been delivered and that tends to mount up against the door – a real give-away to the burglar, especially if there is a glazed panel in the bottom half of your front door.

Installations

LOW-VOLTAGE

A low-voltage outdoor lighting system runs on a 12 or 24 volt supply, normally drawn from a plug-in transformer. This will supply current for several low-wattage lamps, which typically range from 7 to 20 watts. Consequently, their light output will be quite low (when compared to a 60 watt bulb) and the illuminated area quite small. There's an enormous range of low-voltage lighting kits for the garden, which can be used to illuminate a pond, uplight trees and shrubs, or highlight certain features in the garden. They're more suitable for creating an atmospheric mood in the garden than for security, simply because the light output is so low and they have a tendency to cast shadows.

They're very easy and safe to assemble and install, however, and the cabling can be run along the surface of the ground. That said, the cables are thin and easily damaged. While low-voltage lighting will not be capable of actually illuminating an intruder, it will cast his shadow if used to highlight a path or other potential approach route. Ideally, it should be supplemented by a mains system.

MAINS POWERED

A mains powered lighting system runs off the standard domestic 240 volt supply. Protecting the electrical supply to your security lighting is imperative for safety and security reasons, because exposed and unprotected cables can easily be cut. Wherever possible, mount light fittings on the house or outbuilding walls so that power can be supplied through the wall, thus reducing the amount of exposed cabling. If you do intend running exposed cabling, use either mineral-insulated cable (MICC) or bury the cable in heavy-gauge, galvanised steel conduit at least 450 mm (1 ft 6 in) below the ground. Cables in armoured, PVC-sheathed protective plastic conduits must similarly be laid at least 450 mm below the surface to where the point of fixing is reached. If the distance between an outbuilding and the house is less than 3 m (10 ft), PVC-sheathed cable may be run overhead, provided it reaches a minimum height of 3.6 m (12 ft), without the need of additional support or protection.

Any new cabling must come from an isolating mains switch in the house and terminate in the outbuilding or shed at another isolating switch. It should not be wired as an extension from a socket outlet on an outside wall.

For a more sophisticated arrangement, the circuits can be linked to an alarm, so that any attempt at interference will automatically trigger the alarm. For larger dwellings in remote or rural settings, consider installing a back-up system, such as a battery and inverter or stand-by generator. The provision of a non-break system that will ensure an instantaneous change-over in the event of a mains failure can be expensive, but will ensure that the security lighting remains switched on. This is particularly relevant if using high-pressure discharge lamps that have a restrike time.

If you want to install a variety of lights in different locations on and around your property, employing a qualified electrician might be your best option. You should never undertake electrical work yourself unless you know exactly what you're doing. Expect a relatively high cost for the work and some disruption, especially if the cables are to be buried.

MAINTENANCE

Once the security lighting has been installed, it will require a small amount of regular maintenance, such as replacing lamps and cleaning the luminaires. Keep a supply of spare lamps, in case one blows when the shops are shut. Make a periodic check of the fittings and exposed cables for wear and tear and damage, especially before the winter months set in.

Replace blown lamps as soon as possible. Be suspicious of any lamp that appears to have been damaged. While, in most cases, this is likely to be accidental, you should never rule out the possibility that it could have been damaged deliberately.

How to fit an outdoor security light

Outdoor security lighting is a must-have in any home and is sure to deter any intruders – as well as safely welcome callers to your home. To make full and proper use of your new light, make sure it comes on just before the evenings start to draw in at all times of the year.

TOOLS AND MATERIALS

- Existing double socket as near as possible to the front door
- Top quality BS junction box
- Top quality BS FCU – fused connection unit
- Top quality BS light switch
- Outside light – one that is well shielded so that the light is thrown down
- 2 m of 2.5-mm two-core and earth cable

- Pencil and measuring rule
- Short spirit level
- Spike or awl
- Selection of electrical screwdrivers
- Wire strippers and cutters
- Electricians pliers
- Electric drill and drill bits to fit
- Club hammer and cold chisel

IMPORTANT: ALL ELECTRICAL WORK <u>MUST</u> BE CHECKED BY A QUALIFIED ELECTRICIAN

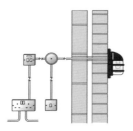

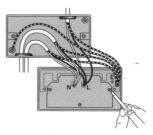

1 ESTABLISHING THE LAYOUT

Have a look at the diagrammatic illustration and see how a spur can be taken from an existing double socket. The layout is as follows: a spur goes up to a switched and fused connection unit, on through a junction box, and then, via a switch, on to the wall light. Screw the new items in place on the walls.

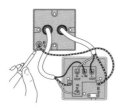

2 WIRING INTO THE EXISTING SOCKET

Switch off the power at the mains, and run a new length of cable into the top of the existing power socket. Strip away the insulation and wire the cores into the appropriate neutral live and earth terminals.

3 WIRING INTO THE FCU AND LIGHT

Run the new cable up from the existing socket into the FCU and connect it to the 'feed' terminals. Run a new length of cable from the 'load' terminals to the switch, the junction box and the light. The light should ideally have a shield at the top to illuminate the face of the caller. Finally switch on the power. **NOTE:** the cables can be hidden in channels cut into the plaster, inside cavity walls or inside plastic ducting.

Locating the lights

AT THE FRONT

A light outside the front door is an essential part of your home security scheme, for if it is positioned correctly, it will illuminate a caller's face and enable you to see them clearly through a door viewer before you open the door. Mount the fitting so that a caller's face will be in full light rather than shadow, which can occur if it is set too high above the door. Use a luminaire that sends out most of its light horizontally and, if possible, fit two lights, one on each side of the door. Remember that you will have to change the lamps and clean the fittings from time to time, so don't make them too high. To reduce the risk of tampering, choose a light fitting that has a screwed on cover.

Sometimes a bright light source at the front door can make other parts of the front of the house or block of flats seem quite dark, so it is sensible to install additional lights in the front garden or hard standing to balance the lighting. This is particularly important if you use a hard standing for parking cars. In this case, if possible, try to illuminate it with a wall or column mounted luminaire so that the light will fall between the cars. Many decorative luminaires are not particularly

efficient at directing light where it's required, so take care when selecting one, especially if its primary purpose is security.

Light coloured surfaces will reflect light far more efficiently than dark ones, which must be taken into account when planning your security lighting.

FLATS

If you live in a block of flats or a house that has been converted into flats, the lighting in the communal areas of the building, including the front path, the entrance door and hall, landings and staircases, should be lit throughout the night. Push-button timed lights are not at all suitable, as they have a habit of going off before you can reach your flat. Some landlords use energy-efficient switching for communal areas. These systems use a passive infra-red detector to turn the lights on for a set time or for as long as movement is detected. They are a good idea, but should increase the lighting from a reduced level used throughout the night, and not simply turn it on and off. The importance of having a door viewer in a private flat entrance door was discussed in Chapter 4; it wouldn't be much use if the hallway outside were in pitch darkness. If the lighting is dim, badly sited or poorly maintained, speak to your neighbours and then make a polite approach to your landlord or managing agent. Show him a copy of this book and a print-out of the guidance notes for 'New Housing' from the Secured by Design website, which sets out the minimum lighting requirements for flats.

It may be possible to install your own additional light fittings, but you must get

---

ESSENTIAL ADVICE

Do not attempt to install any electrical system unless you have the necessary skills and knowledge to undertake the work. Most lighting equipment sold in DIY stores is packaged with plenty of information to help you install it, but if in any doubt, call in a qualified electrician or lighting engineer.

SAFETY NOTE

Over 150,000 people are injured each year on garden paths and steps. Some of these accidents are almost certainly the result of poor or inadequate lighting. When installing lighting around your home, take care not to create a hazard for any of your family or friends.

A person using a path lit by a PIR controlled lamp may suddenly be thrown into total darkness once out of its field of detection, increasing the risk of stumbling. Similarly, a floodlight at the bottom of a flight of stairs can temporarily blind a person descending.

the landlord's permission first (*see also Chap 1*).

In the majority of cases, well-positioned lights at the main entrance will be sufficient to throw some light along the front path or drive. If this is long, some additional lighting would be useful, provided it is balanced by extra lighting in the garden or on any hard standing to the side. This is because if you are near a bright light, you may not be able to see beyond it. Additional lighting can be provided by bollard lights (preferably with caps to prevent upward and sometimes dazzling light spill) or column (post) mounted lights. For very long paths and drives, column lighting will maximise coverage, although the total amount will be determined by the output of the lamp, the height of the column and the way the luminaire's reflector directs the light. This work is best undertaken by a qualified lighting engineer, and a number of consultants can be found on the Institution of Lighting Engineers website (*see Useful Contacts, opposite*).

STREET LIGHTING

If you are lucky enough (some might say unlucky) to have a street lamp right outside your home, do not be tempted to consider it as part of your security lighting, because you will have no control over it. While you can call the council to let them know that the lamp isn't working, it could be a few days before they repair it, and the front of your home would be in darkness for all of that time.

TO THE BACK AND SIDE

Security lighting seems to work best when it is matched with the potential for clear observation from your own property and neighbouring properties. The thief has to feel vulnerable, so there is very little advantage in lighting an area that can't be overlooked. Bear this in mind when planning your lighting and security improvements, and try to combine the two. In Chapter 3, it was suggested that any side gate should be designed so that it provides a view along the side of the house or block of flats, just in case a burglar manages to climb over it. Using a light in this situation is advantageous, because you are illuminating a space that is easily seen from the street. If the gate is solid, it's best to place the light directly above it, so that any attempt to climb it at night will be more visible from the street. The light outside a glazed back or side door should be positioned carefully so that the light source can't be seen from indoors. Bear in mind that a light located on a corner will illuminate two elevations at once.

GARAGES AND OUTBUILDINGS

If your garage has an up-and-over door,

it's not a good idea to install a light immediately above the door, as the door may cast a shadow when opened, preventing reflected light from entering the garage. Sheds and greenhouses can be fitted with lights or illuminated by spotlights from more convenient locations.

LIGHTING AND SOUND TOGETHER

This chapter has recommended that you operate some of your internal lights on timers to give the impression that you are at home when, in fact, you are out. You can enhance this 'evidence of occupancy' using a pre-recorded sound product called AudioGuard. AudioGuard is a set of four digitally-engineered CDs carrying sounds of random domestic activity. You simply place the CD in any CD player, press Play and Repeat and let the noises begin. The sounds include the noise of builders, vacuum cleaners, cutlery, microwaves and so on, but not voices as it was thought they would be too easily recognisable. Some of the sounds included are deliberately designed to be threatening to the intruder, yet unthreatening to the householder, such as the growling of a dog. Do make sure you inform the neighbours if you use this product to avoid embarrassing calls to the police!

USEFUL CONTACTS
AudioGuard
www.audioguard.com

D.W. Windsor
www.dwwindsor.co.uk

Eminent Plus Lighting
(Tel: 01753 534888 Fax: 01753 573275)

Institution of Lighting Engineers
www.ile.org.uk

CHAPTER 7

Electronic security

Intruder alarm system

There are many myths about whether alarm systems actually do deter burglars. It used to be said that only the well-off could afford a system, and that a house displaying an alarm bell box indicated that there was something worth stealing. Consequently, some people were reluctant to have systems installed for fear of encouraging burglars. Thankfully, these myths have been dispelled by the findings of the British Crime Survey, which show that intruder alarm systems do reduce the likelihood of burglary.

That said, some still see the house alarm as more of an irritation than a security improvement, a view prompted by the sheer number of false alarms from many systems. The cost has also deterred people from buying them, even though, in reality, their price has probably never been more competitive nor their operation so easy. The fact is that alarm boxes on the front and back of a house are likely to deter the majority of determined thieves, and even if they don't, at least your neighbour's attention will be drawn to your house when the alarm does go off.

It is important to understand that an intruder alarm should not be installed instead of taking physical measures to secure your home, as described in previous chapters. Rather, it should be seen as a means of summoning help if those physical measures are overcome. The alarm must not place any restrictions on your movements within the home, nor have an adverse effect on your daily routines, apart from having to turn it on and off.

TYPES OF ALARM SYSTEM

Essentially, there are three types of alarm system, ranging from the inexpensive DIY kit, through the audible system that is usually professionally installed, to the monitored system, which sends a signal down a telephone line to a central monitoring station. Most alarms are 'hard wired', which means that each detector is physically connected by wire to the control panel. In a DIY wired system, the wiring is usually colour coded with clear and concise instructions on how to install the alarm. A number of wire-free systems are available, which rely on tiny radio transmitters and receivers to communicate between the detectors and the control panel. Wire-free systems are the simplest DIY solution, as they are easy to install, require no cabling and cause the minimum of disruption in the home.

The principle components are similar for all types of alarm system. Each will have a control panel and a number of detectors. When the alarm is activated, it normally operates an internal or external sounder (or both) in the form of a siren, most bell systems having been replaced years ago. The majority of systems are powered from the domestic mains electrical supply and have a battery back-up in case of power failure. The most popular type of house alarm is the basic audible version, which activates an external sounder (bell box) to call attention to the house. At the same time, it triggers a very loud, ear piercing internal sounder, usually placed near the control panel, to encourage the burglar to leave.

IMPORTANT CONSIDERATIONS

When installing an audible alarm, an important consideration is your neighbours' reaction if it goes off, as you will be relying on them to look out of the window to see what's happening and to notify the police on your behalf. Equally important is your choice of a keyholder, someone who can be contacted by telephone and who is willing, no matter what time of the day or night, to attend the premises in response to the alarm going off. They must have their own transport so that they can get there within 20 minutes of being called. They should also have a good knowledge of your home and be fully conversant with the operation of the alarm, so that they can turn it off and reset it. Council environmental health departments offer a free keyholder registration service, and will contact a keyholder on a householder's behalf if they are away on holiday, etc.

Noise from domestic audible intruder alarms often results in complaints to local authorities. If an alarm is activated, it may cause a disturbance to neighbours for some time. However, if an alarm continues to sound for more than 20 minutes, and the environmental health office is satisfied that the noise is causing a statutory nuisance, formal action may be taken to silence it. This involves obtaining a warrant from a Magistrates Court to enter the premises, and the employment of specialist contractors to gain access, deactivate the alarm and, if necessary, change the locks to leave the house secure. The cost of carrying out such work, which can run into hundreds of pounds, can be recovered from the householder.

The following steps will help to minimise the risk of an alarm causing problems to your neighbours:

- Make sure the alarm is fitted with a 20-minute cut-out device.

- Have the alarm serviced regularly.

- Provide your local authority with details of keyholders who can be contacted if the alarm sounds while you are away from home (especially if you are on holiday).

- Tell your neighbours how to get hold of the keyholders.

If you live in a fairly isolated location, or don't want to involve your neighbours, or want to ensure attendance at your home to investigate the cause of the alarm going off, you could opt for a remotely monitored system. This ensures that someone other than your neighbours will know what has happened. The monitoring service will automatically call a keyholder (which could be a security guarding company) and the police.

Alarm systems that do not conform to police requirements outlined in this chapter will not receive a police response unless reported by a person at the premises reporting a crime or suspicion of a crime in progress. Full details of police requirements may be found at www.securedbydesign.com or from your local police headquarters.

A centrally monitored alarm can be designed to allow staff at the monitoring station to see and hear what is going on in the building if the alarm is activated. This type of system is known as a 'confirmed alarm'. Although more expensive than a basic audible alarm, a confirmed alarm is the only type that guarantees the attendance of the police following a call from the monitoring station. All monitored alarms to which the police are called must be authenticated by sequential, visual or audible confirmation. Visually confirmed systems have small cameras at various locations around the building, or within the detectors, enabling the monitoring station to see an intruder or a suspect vehicle in the grounds of the property. Audio confirmed systems use microphones to listen to any activity within the premises after activation of the alarm. Sequentially confirmed systems look for successive tripping of individual detectors, which would indicate movement within the building.

There are a number of British and European standards for intruder alarms, which govern the manufacture of the components, the installation and the operation. BS 4737 – more recently replaced by BSEN 50131-1 – is the most familiar of the standards for normal hard-wired domestic systems; BS 7042 is the standard for high-security systems; and BS 6799 class 6 is the standard for wire-free systems. These are being replaced by BSEN 50131, a new European Standard.

If you are considering having an alarm installed professionally, note that the police will only accept the installation of remote signalling alarms by companies that conform to the Association of Chief Police Officers (ACPO) security systems policy, and whose business is subject to inspection by an independent body accredited to UKAS (United Kingdom Accreditation Service). Currently, only two organisations are accepted by the police:

- The National Security Inspectorate (NSI)

- The Security Systems and Alarm Inspection Board (SSAIB).

POLICE RECOGNITION OF ALARM COMPANIES

NSI and SSAIB publish a list of companies considered to be compliant under the police policy. However, the fact that a company has its details on the list does not necessarily mean that the company or its work have been inspected by the police. Consumers should ask installers for confirmation that they have police recognition, or alternatively contact the Alarms Administrator at your local police headquarters.

Basically, any company that is listed may install and maintain remote signalling alarm systems within that police area. The alarm company must apply to the chief officer of police to install a security system requiring a Police Unique Reference Number (URN). The police will charge the customer an administration fee for this. It may be paid via the installer. While this process is under way, any activation of the alarm will not receive a police response (*see opposite*) until the Unique Reference Number has been issued.

If a company loses its police recognition, its existing customers have 12 months in which to make alternative arrangements for maintenance and monitoring.

To be included on the list, an alarm company must be inspected by one of the independent bodies mentioned previously. The company must not employ anyone in its surveying, sales, installation or maintenance departments who has a criminal conviction, and the personnel are subjected to a criminal records check.

Details of intruder alarms will be held on a computer, and an alarm company will have to inform its clients of that fact, although only a limited amount of data is supplied to the police. This must include details of any hazards at the premises, such as swimming pools, hazardous chemicals stored or similar that may be a risk to officers attending. The information supplied has to be accurate and kept up to date; it is the alarm company's responsibility to notify the police of any changes, which must be done within 14 days.

ALARM RECEIVING CENTRES

The police do not accept calls from dedicated telephone lines linked to remote signalling alarm systems. Years ago, there were automatic diallers that had equipment linked to local police stations, and if activated, they would attract an automatic police response. You can still buy a variation of this type of automatic dialling device, which plays a message down the line. However, they do not qualify under the police service intruder alarm policy. They will not receive a police response and must not be programmed to dial 999 or police stations.

An alarm receiving centre reports alarm activations from remote signalling systems that require a police response.

On receiving an activation through a dedicated telephone line, they immediately contact the control room of the relevant police service, giving the system's URN. From this, the police can determine the location of the premises, whether there are any known health or safety risks associated with them, and details on the level of response required.

POLICE RESPONSE

Every year, the police respond to thousands of alarms calls, many of which turn out to be false activations – perhaps because a keyholder is late in locking up and has forgotten the alarm code, or because a bird has flown in through an open skylight and in front of a detector. While the police acknowledge that mistakes will occur, the idea behind monitored alarm systems is to reduce the number of false-call incidents. Ultimately, the police response is determined by the nature of demand, priorities and the resources available at the time of a request for assistance. Therefore, a stringent code of practice exists in respect of police response; currently, there are three levels:

Level 1 Immediate
The police respond as soon as possible.

Level 2
Police response is desirable, but attendance may be delayed depending on available resources. The police response is managed and is dependant upon available information.

Level 3
No police attendance; keyholder response only.

In the case of alarm systems issued with a URN, the police will continue to offer Level 1 response until such time as they receive two false calls in a rolling 12-month period. After that, they move the response to Level 2. If the number of false calls increases to five within the same 12-month period, it is downgraded to Level 3 and police response is withdrawn. Following the withdrawal of police response, a minimum of three months must pass with no further false calls before consideration is given to restoring the response. The original cause of the false activation must be rectified before the process can begin again. If the level of false calls delays the restoration of response for more than six months, the URN is deleted, and the customer and security company have to apply for a new URN.

ACTIVE MONITORING

When you have a monitored alarm system, the signal that is sent down the telephone line to the central monitoring station can also be checked to ensure that the line is active and working. BT Redcare is an intelligent alarm signalling service that guarantees the alarm signal will reach the monitoring station. It uses your existing telephone line, to which is connected a small attachment (Modem Compatible Device). This actively checks that the line is fully operational. If the line is cut or tampered with, the device sends a signal directly to Redcare.

Redcare GSM employs two alarm monitoring paths: radio signal and telephone line. If one of the paths is attacked, the other continues to monitor for any further alarms, transmitting them as confirmed activations.

PERSONAL ATTACK ALARM

Most intruder systems cater for a personal attack alarm. This is normally operated to summon urgent police assistance when someone enters a building, usually a pre-defined area of it, with the intention of threatening or harming an occupant. It must be said that such incidents are very rare, although incorporating panic buttons into an intruder alarm system is commonplace.

Panic buttons are usually fitted near the front door and in the master bedroom, although the majority of alarm companies should discuss your specific needs in this respect. You can also have a portable device, which allows greater flexibility, but it must be capable of transmitting its exact location.

Where an alarm system incorporates both personal attack and intruder detection equipment, the remote signal differentiates between the two types of activation. Most people would want a Level 1 response to a personal attack alarm and, if this is the case, both the intruder and personal attack alarms will need their own URNs. Thus, the police will automatically be made aware of the type of incident they are attending.

The policing of personal attack alarms is subject to the same code of practice as intruder alarms. However, the police response following five false calls to the system may vary in some police forces and you should check local procedures with the Alarms Administrator at police headquarters.

IMPORTANT POINTS TO CONSIDER

Here are ten considerations and questions to ask a security company before deciding on a particular alarm system:

1. Arrange an appointment that suits you. Allow yourself plenty of time to discuss the security of your home. Do not be in a rush.

2. If the installation of an alarm is a requirement of your insurance company, is the company acceptable to your insurer?

3. Before disclosing any personal details, check the address and credentials of the company, and satisfy yourself as to the credentials of the company's representative.

4. Is the company subjected to an independent inspection process and, if so, which organisation?

5. Will the company representative provide a list of police rules for occupiers of premises with alarms, and written confirmation that both the alarm and the company are currently acceptable to the local police for the transmission of alarm messages from new installations?

6. Does the alarm system reach the required British/European Standard? Tell the installer that you require the alarm to conform to BS 4737, BSEN 50131-1 or BS 7042 (high-security systems), or for wire-free alarms, BS 6799 or European equivalent.

7. Does the company offer a rented system or will you own it? Are there monitoring costs and/or hidden extras?

8. Is there a 24-hour call-out service and emergency attendance within four hours?

9. Is there a guarantee with the system? If so, how long does it last and what happens if there is a problem after the guarantee expires?

10. Does the installing company provide adequate training in the operation of the system, and what happens if you become confused and need more training?

Take the time to read any agreements carefully before signing. Don't accept verbal contracts. If you are unsure, have the contract checked by a legal professional. For further advice, you can contact the security systems office at your regional police headquarters, or your local crime reduction officer.

ALARMS FOR OUTBUILDINGS

It is possible to install an alarm system in most outbuildings, but a wooden shed containing a lawnmower, tools and a couple of bicycles may not warrant the expense. A professional installer would advise extending a full house alarm system into a substantial outbuilding, such as a brick built garage or workshop, but should not do so for a wooden shed. However, there is a solution to the problem of wooden sheds and similar less-sturdy structures. You can buy battery operated or plug-in self-contained alarms from most DIY stores and security shops. The battery operated types normally comprise a mechanical switch and a 120-decibel sounder, whereas the plug-in units combine the sounder with a passive infra-red detector.

COMMUNITY ALARMS FOR THE ELDERLY

In some areas, Help the Aged operate a community alarm system that is managed by the Senior Link bogus caller scheme. This provides a 24-hour immediate response service for vulnerable older people. Senior Link installs a radio triggered base unit and pendant or door alert button, which can be pressed if a suspicious caller is at the door. Pressing the button causes the unit to call the Senior Link Response Centre. A trained operator answers the call, and simultaneously the client's details are displayed on a computer screen, indicating that help is needed. The operator can offer advice and support, and make any necessary calls to check the identity of the caller or summon the police. Help the Aged also operates a Handy Van Scheme, making older people's homes safer and more secure.

CLOSED-CIRCUIT TELEVISION

Miniature closed-circuit television (CCTV) cameras are widely available, allowing you to protect your property whether you are at home or away. The cameras can be mounted on house walls or lighting columns to monitor specific vulnerable areas, including the back garden, side access, shed, garage and approach to the front door. Not only do cameras act as a visual deterrent for intruders, but also they allow you to see visitors approaching the property.

A domestic CCTV system usually comprises one or two weatherproof cameras, an adaptor and a television monitor. The cameras can also be connected to a video recorder and television. This allows you to view your garden from your armchair at the touch of a button. Cameras can be movement activated so that they automatically change the TV channel to show the camera picture when movement is detected. Similarly, if the cameras are linked to your home video recorder, it will automatically record the images produced. The more adventurous can

even link a camera system to a home computer, enabling you to fully automate recordings.

Such systems are particularly good for the elderly and disabled, who need to be able to see and recognise callers at the front door. In addition, a CCTV camera will allow you to keep an eye on your children while getting on with other tasks.

Miniature closed-circuit television monitor

If CCTV cameras are to be effective, you must provide a good level of light in the garden at night. Also, cameras must not look beyond the boundary of your property, although their use on domestic dwellings does not require them to be registered under the codes of practice of the Data Protection Act.

PERIMETER DETECTION SYSTEMS

The vast majority of family homes do not extend beyond the average-size plot and, therefore, won't require a sophisticated perimeter detection system. However, such systems do exist and are designed

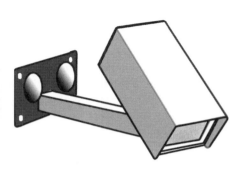

Closed-circuit camera in
weather-proof housing

to detect the entry of an intruder into an
outdoor area that requires protection. This
type of system identifies the location of
the intrusion and sends a signal to an
alarm. Perimeter detection systems must
be installed professionally. The principle
form of detection used comprises special
detecting cables that are attached to the
perimeter fence or buried underground.
Microwaves and active infra-red beams
sent from a transmitter to a receiver can
also operate such systems. If the beam
is interrupted, the alarm is activated.
Basically, the system forms an invisible
'fence' of detection just within the
perimeter.

USEFUL CONTACTS
Help the Aged
207–221 Pentonville Road
London N1 9UZ
(020 7278 1114)
seniorsafety@helptheaged.org.uk

Local police headquarters
www.police.uk
(gives access to Police Force map and
contacts)

**National Security Inspectorate
(NSI)**
Queensgate House
14 Cookham Road
Maidenhead
Berkshire SL6 8AJ
(Tel: 0870 205 0000 or 01628 37512
Fax: 01628 773367)

Redcare Security
www.redcare.bt.com

**Security Systems and Alarm
Inspection Board (SSAIB)**
Suite 3
131 Bedford Street
North Shields
Tyne & Wear NE29 6LA
(Tel: 0191 296 3242
Fax: 0191 296 2667)

Senstar Stellar Limited (outdoor
perimeter security)
www.senstarstellar.com

CHAPTER 8

Personal safety

Although this book is primarily about the security of your home and garden, it's sensible to take steps to protect yourself when you're out and about. Everyone should be able to live life freely, to come and go as they please, by day or night, without fear of being attacked. But that doesn't mean that you shouldn't be prepared for the unexpected. Even witnessing an attack on someone else can have a very traumatic effect. No one wants to fill their mind with unpleasant thoughts, but it is important to think ahead; consider what you would do in the event of an attack, so that you are aware of your surroundings and can go about your everyday life with confidence. Simple forward planning and common-sense precautions can do much to ensure your personal safety.

Although the media make much of unusual and shocking crimes of violence, particularly involving the elderly, it is important to realise that such incidents are rare, which is why they are newsworthy. Crime stories are very important to the media and can often account for up to 40 per cent of a newspaper's entire editorial content. The danger, however, is that this gives an unrealistic picture of the situation. It is important not to let a fear of crime get out of hand.

Going out

People are far more likely to take reasonable steps to travel safely when they are out late at night and on their own. Parents nag teenagers about making sure they can get home safely, either by sharing a lift with a friend or by checking bus and train timetables, or booking a taxi in advance. But parents may not necessarily follow the same rules. We tend to be creatures of habit, using, for example, the same trusted taxi firm. That's all very well if you're close to home, but what if you are in unfamiliar surroundings? In this situation, make sure you use a licensed taxi. Check that it carries its licence plates and that the driver displays his permit inside the vehicle. When you phone to book a cab, ask for the driver's name and call sign so that you can verify his identity when he arrives. Where you sit in the vehicle is a matter of choice. Most people tend to sit in the back, but some prefer to sit in the front where they feel they have more control of the situation. Trust your instincts; if you have any doubts, don't get into a cab, and if you begin to become worried during the journey, get the driver to drop you in the nearest busy place.

Never accept a lift from anyone you've only just met, no matter how genuine they seem. This may prove difficult, especially if you really like them and want to get to know them better. It's better to be safe than sorry, so ask for their telephone number and arrange to call or text them. Arrange to meet them on neutral ground, where there are plenty of other people, until you feel confident to be alone with them.

If you walk home alone at night, avoid short-cuts through dimly lit areas and open ground. Always walk in the centre of the pavement, keeping well away from bushes, dark alleyways and recesses. If possible, walk facing oncoming traffic; this makes it difficult for a kerb crawler to follow you. Walk at a good pace with a sense of purpose, holding your head up and looking well ahead. In this way, you will see any potential trouble looming ahead and will have plenty of time to cross the road if necessary. And men, please consider how a lone woman might feel, so rather than walk behind her, cross the road.

If you are keen on keeping fit and enjoy running in the evenings after work, choose well-populated routes. Avoid using a personal stereo. Not only will it prevent you from hearing anyone approaching, but also it could leave you vulnerable to a snatch thief.

Cover up expensive jewellery when you go out, and if you carry a handbag, hold it close to your body. If possible, downsize your handbag by only taking the real essentials with you. Keep your house keys in a coat, jacket or trouser pocket, rather than in a handbag. That way, if the bag is stolen, you will be able to get back into your home. Purses should always be pushed to the bottom of a bag to guard against pickpockets, while men should resist the temptation to carry their wallet in a back trouser pocket. Don't leave briefcases, suitcases or any other bags unattended; keep them close to you at all times. This is particularly relevant on public transport and at railway stations, where the threat of terrorism is always lurking at the back of our minds. Be particularly careful when checking into a hotel, because bag theft from hotel receptions is commonplace, especially in the cities. Always make use of a room safe or a deposit safe in reception to store any items of value such as jewellery, a camera, cash or passports.

PUBLIC TRANSPORT

If travelling alone on public transport, try to avoid using isolated bus stops and railway stations. If possible, arrange for someone to pick you up from your destination. On buses, sit nearest the driver; on trains, try to avoid empty compartments and carriages, and those with any dubious looking characters. Most people travelling on trains late at night are usually relaxed and friendly individuals, but women who find themselves alone in a compartment with a man on his own should move to another compartment if they feel ill at ease. Some men can find it just as difficult in these circumstances, and may often help a woman feel safer by moving to another seat or compartment themselves.

PERSONAL ATTACK ALARM

Many women feel safer when carrying a personal alarm. In the event of an attack, it can be activated to produce an ear piercing screech, which should frighten off any would-be attacker. It may also alert someone nearby that there's a problem, but its main strength lies in the sudden noise it makes, which will help you surprise an attacker and escape. Alarms may be gas or battery operated, and can be bought at any DIY store. Gas operated alarms are louder, but make sure you choose one with a press-top that locks into place, so that it will sound continuously even if knocked from your hand. Shaking the gas bottle will usually tell you if there is plenty of gas left, but check the manufacturer's instructions as to the life of the product and replace it in plenty of time. Battery operated personal attack alarms are often combined with

Battery-operated personal attack alarm

Gas-powered personal attack alarm

torches, which are very useful. Make sure you check the batteries at regular intervals. It is essential to know how to operate your alarm instinctively, and to be aware of the sound it makes so that you're not the one who is surprised. Don't push it to the bottom of a handbag and forget about it. Keep it easily to hand, and if you're on your own walking along a street, hold it in your hand in a coat pocket.

Safety in the car

Most people rely on their cars for daily transport, but other than filling them with petrol and occasionally checking the oil, water and tyre pressures, don't give them a second thought. Do you, for example, know if your car's horn works without the ignition being switched on?

Although it is common sense, make sure that your car is serviced regularly and that you have enough fuel for your journey. A surprising number of people set off, only to run out of petrol before they reach their destination. Then they call the police or one of the breakdown recovery services for roadside assistance, a situation that could have been avoided so easily by a little forethought.

If your car is playing up, find an alternative means of transport; don't be tempted to take a chance. If you're making a long journey or driving to an unfamiliar area, plan your route in advance. If you're not very good at map reading, consider using your computer to download a route from a route planning website. Most are very simple to use, only requiring you to type in your address and postcode, and the details of your destination and its postcode. The route planner selects the most appropriate route (shortest in mileage or quickest using motorways), giving you step-by-step directions. Bear in mind, however, that the route won't necessarily allow for road works or diversions, so always carry an up-to-date road atlas with you as a back-up. Keep the atlas inside the vehicle, not in the boot, so that you can refer to it easily. Always carry some loose change in case you have to make a phone call; if you have a mobile phone, make sure you use a hands-free kit when driving. Don't forget that it is an offence to drive and use a mobile phone that is not hands-free.

IF YOU BREAK DOWN

If your car breaks down, pull over as far to the left of the carriageway as you can; if possible, coast the vehicle to the most convenient spot. Always let someone know where you are and that you have broken down. If you are on a major road and the traffic is busy, apart from making the initial phone call, follow the advice given below.

If you break down on a motorway, always use one of the phones at the side of the carriageway, as it will give the police control room your exact location. They are sited a mile apart, so you'll always be within half a mile of one. Look for the arrows on the marker posts at the side of the motorway, which will point in the direction of the nearest phone. Again, if possible, coast the vehicle to the nearest phone.

Although motorways are the safest type of road to travel on, they are still potentially dangerous places to be,

especially if you're sitting on the hard shoulder. Unfortunately, drivers who are tired or otherwise inattentive do wander on to the hard shoulder, resulting in a number of fatalities every year. For safety, get out of the car and stay out of it, and once you've made your call for assistance, walk up the bank or get as far from the hard shoulder as you can. Be very careful when getting out of the vehicle, especially from the driver's side, as you'll be close to fast moving traffic. If possible, get out on the passenger side of the car (or the side closest to the side of the road). If you have to walk to a phone, keep to the innermost side of the hard shoulder, or preferably off the roadway altogether, and keep young children with you. Never be tempted to cross to the other side of a dual carriageway or motorway because, apart from being dangerous, most emergency phones tend to be opposite each other anyway. Making a call from a roadside phone may prove difficult because busy motorways are very noisy environments, so be prepared to shout. Always make your call while facing the oncoming traffic, just in case a vehicle wanders on to the hard shoulder. If you have no choice but to stay in the car, sit in the front passenger seat with your seatbelt on until assistance arrives.

Always inform the emergency services if you or one of your passengers are disabled, you are a lone woman or there are young children with you, as your request for assistance will be given priority. The response from the motoring organisations, such as the AA and RAC, is very efficient, and it really does pay to join one, especially if you do break down on a motorway and need to be towed off. The alternative will be to use the duty recovery service called out by the police, which will only tow your car to the nearest garage. This can be expensive, and you still have the additional problem of getting your car moved either to your local garage or to your home.

SECURITY PRECAUTIONS

Never pick up hitchhikers. If someone flags you down, make sure it is a genuine emergency before winding down the window completely or unlocking the door. When driving an open-topped car in town, make sure personal property, such as a handbag, mobile phone or wallet, are not sitting on a passenger seat. Some saloon convertibles have demountable windbreaks that sit over the back seats when they are not in use. If the back seats are unoccupied, use the windbreak and leave your personal property in the foot wells in front of the back seats. If you pull up behind another vehicle, always leave plenty of room in case you need to drive around it. Normally, if you can clearly see the bottoms of the back tyres of the vehicle in front, you'll be at the right distance. When driving in towns, keep your doors locked. Place handbags out of sight or on the floor; do not leave them on the front passenger seat where they could easily be snatched.

If you think another vehicle is following you, reduce your speed, check that your doors are locked and avoid making eye contact with its occupants. Drive to the nearest police station if you know where it is or to a busy place such as a petrol station, or to a busy street where there are plenty of people about. Slow right down (but don't stop), sound the horn and flash your lights.

Some young people like to cruise about town playing loud music and spinning their tyres. Although, for the most part, they just want to have a little fun, this can annoy other drivers and sometimes intimidate them, especially at traffic lights where they will sit revving their engines. It's important in this situation to keep cool and avoid eye contact, especially if they are obviously aggressive. In recent years, there has been an increase in 'road rage' incidents, so don't be tempted to pull a face or make a rude gesture. Instead, if you've witnessed a serious piece of dangerous driving, try to record the registration of the offending car and details of the location, then report the matter to the police. Don't let the occupants of the other car see you do this.

Missing from home

A child going missing is a parent's worst nightmare. Thankfully, however, in nearly every case, the child turns up safe and well. People are a little reticent about contacting the police when they believe a loved one is missing, often because they're not too sure when they should call. The timing of a call is a matter of conjecture, as it depends very much on the circumstances and the vulnerability of the child or missing person. A baby or a very young child could be regarded as missing if they've been gone for a few seconds, and you would call the police immediately. An older child, who has not come home from a friend's house on time, could be cause for concern if they're 30 minutes late. Teenagers often lose track of time and don't show up for dinner, and some are not too keen on being held to a time limit. These 'no shows' often lead to a parent making a call to the child's mobile phone, followed by a text message when there's no reply. Subsequently, they call the child's friends' homes, then start walking and driving around nearby streets. This reaction to someone going missing is quite normal.

The golden rule is to call the police as soon as you become concerned and you have checked all the obvious places. The police would far rather be called straight away, so that initial checks can be made, than receive a call several hours later with only sketchy information to act on. Having done this, there's no reason not to continue contacting friends, etc.

The police will treat your call very seriously, and an officer will visit you to collect more information about the incident, and obtain a recent photograph and a full description of the child's clothing. Don't be surprised if the officer asks to search your home and garden, as this is a very routine initial check. 'Missing' children have often been found stuck in trees, sitting in the family car listening to the radio or hiding in cupboards. The police grade missing-person incidents according to the circumstances of each case, but if a child is involved, the matter will be given the utmost importance. A family member will always be asked to stay at home in case the child gets in contact.

So remember, if you are worried about anyone who is missing from home, no matter what their age, or are in any doubt about their whereabouts, call the police.

USEFUL CONTACTS
Advice for Students
www.good2bsecure.gov.uk

Commission for Racial Equality
www.cre.gov.uk

Government Advice
www.crimereduction.gov.uk/ypgcp05.htm
www.scotland.gov.uk/clickthinking/default.htm

Homophobic Hate Crime
www.rainbownetwork.com

Mobile Phone Crime
www.immobilise.com
www.menduk.org

National Neighbourhood Watch Association
www.ukwatch.org.uk

Personal Safety for Children
www.kidscape.org.uk

Rape Crisis
www.rapecrisis.co.uk

Suzy Lamplugh Trust (The)
www.suzylamplugh.org

Victim Support
www.victimsupport.org.uk

CHAPTER 9

Useful legal information

Environmental health

Environmental health and public protection officers are employed by local authorities and provide a very important service to the public. Their job is to remove or control anything that has an adverse effect on our health and well-being, both at home and at work. In addition, they are required to educate and advise the general public on environmental issues. One of the most common complaints they deal with is noise nuisance.

NOISE NUISANCE

Excessive and unwanted noise is a consequence of modern life. A neighbour who constantly has a stereo blaring out all day and half the night can certainly cause annoyance, and even ill health. If the noise is deemed to be a nuisance, the council can take legal action to suppress it.

TRAVELLERS

There are many purpose built traveller sites throughout the country, but some travellers continue to camp on private and publicly owned land. This can be very frustrating if they happen to pull up on land directly outside your property. Unfortunately, having stayed in a place for a week or two, they may leave behind a great deal of litter and damage for others to clear up and repair, the bill often being picked up by the local authority. Once a council is aware of an intrusion by travellers on to their land, the environmental health and public services department will normally act quickly through the courts to obtain an order of possession. This usually takes three or four days, after which the council, often working with the police, will evict the travellers.

To find out more about local government public services, including action taken on environmental issues and safer communities, see *Useful Contacts, p 167.*

Health and safety

As a homeowner, you are not subject to health and safety legislation. However, if you employ someone to carry out any building or construction work on your home, there may be requirements under the Construction (Design and Management) Regulations 1994 (CDM). 'CDM' is a code of practice intended to protect the health and safety of people working in construction, and anyone else who uses the premises and who may be affected by their work. It also covers the maintenance of the building and its eventual demolition or dismantling. If, for example, you have a home extension built, the contractor is responsible for ensuring that anyone working on the building is adequately protected and that safe working practices are adopted. They must make sure that there is a safe route in and out of the premises. They are also responsible for your safety while the work is in progress and for the safety of any visitors who call at your home. Before you build or alter your home, make sure you understand the building regulations and the planning process. You can find more information in *Home Conversions – The Complete Handbook* by Paul Hymers (New Holland Publishers, ISBN 1 84330 352 3).

Definitions of offences

The police receive tens of thousands of calls from the public each year, reporting crimes they have either witnessed or have suffered. Sometimes, however, callers are not exactly sure about the type of offence that may have been committed or, indeed, whether a crime has been committed at all. For this reason, the more common types of offence are given here.

With the exception of common assault, all the crimes listed are known as 'arrestable offences'. An arrestable offence is one where the sentence has been fixed by law, e.g. murder, or is an offence for which you could receive five years imprisonment or more on a first conviction, e.g. burglary; or which has been declared arrestable by statute (e.g. 'offensive weapon').

TACKLING CRIMINALS – REASONABLE FORCE

Anyone may arrest, without warrant, a person who is in the act of committing an arrestable offence; a person they have reasonable grounds to suspect is committing an offence; a person they know is guilty of committing an arrestable offence; or a person for whom they have reasonable grounds to suspect is guilty. If in doubt or concerned for your safety, call the police. You can help by providing a statement and attending court, for without this information, the police may not be able to prosecute.

Recent public concern about what force you can use when confronted by burglars has led the Crown Prosecution Service (CPS) to release the following advice:

'Anyone can use reasonable force to protect themselves or others, or to carry out an arrest, or to prevent crime. You are not expected to make fine judgements over the level of force you use in the heat of the moment. So long as you only do what you honestly and instinctively believe is necessary in the heat of the moment that would be the strongest evidence of you acting lawfully and in self-defence. This is still the case if you use something to hand as a weapon.' Normally 'the more extreme the circumstances and the fear felt, the more force you can lawfully use in self-defence.'

When in your home 'the law does not require you to wait to be attacked before using defensive force yourself.' If an intruder dies you would still have acted lawfully if 'you acted in reasonable self-defence.' However, if, having knocked an intruder unconscious, you decided to further hurt or kill them; or you knew of an intended burglary into your home and set a trap to hurt or kill them rather than involve the police you would be acting with excessive and gratuitous force and could be prosecuted.'

If you chase after them you may use reasonable force to arrest the intruder or recover your property. 'A rugby tackle or single blow would probably be reasonable. Acting out of malice and revenge with the intent of inflicting punishment through injury or death would not.' (see Useful Contacts, p 167)

CRIMINAL DAMAGE

An offence of criminal damage is committed when a person, without lawful excuse, deliberately destroys or damages any property belonging to someone else, or behaves recklessly, causing the property to be destroyed or damaged.

The words 'vandalism' and 'vandal' are often used in the context of criminal damage, although not generally by the police. Everyone should be wary about incidents of criminal damage, as if left unreported, it can lead to even more serious damage in the future.

THREAT TO COMMIT CRIMINAL DAMAGE

This concerns someone who, without lawful excuse, makes a threat against another person, with the intention that they should fear that the threat would be carried out. The threat can be to destroy or damage any property belonging to that person, or to another, just so long as the person receiving the threat genuinely believes the act would be carried out. In addition, a person is also guilty of the offence if they destroy or damage their own property in a manner that they know to be likely to endanger the life of the person threatened or a third person.

There are two important points to consider. One is that the threat must be to another person, but can relate to a third party. For example, 'I'll smash up your daughter's car if you don't do what I say.' The other is that the offence is also committed if the offender threatens to damage his own property to endanger the life of another. An example of this would be a landlord threatening to burn down his own pub if the tenant manager won't leave.

THEFT

A person is guilty of theft if they dishonestly appropriate property belonging to another with the intention of depriving them of it permanently. Property includes money, and also things

in action and other intangible items, such as deeds to a property. It does not include land, except in circumstances where some action has been taken to sever it. Examples of this would be a neighbour removing topsoil from your garden, or a tenant in a Housing Association Property removing something that is attached to the land, a window or door from the home perhaps. The doors and windows are considered part of the fixtures and fitting of the property on the land.

Appropriation means any assumption by a person of the rights of an owner, whereupon he deals with it and treats it as his own, whether he came by the property (innocently or not) without stealing it and then later decided to treat it as the owner.

Permanently depriving means that the person who takes the property has absolutely no intention of giving it back.

There are many different words that sum up the meaning of dishonesty. However, dishonesty does not apply in circumstances where a person believes they have a lawful right to property, or if they took the property believing that they would have been given consent if the owner had known of the circumstances. It also does not apply if someone appropriates the property in the belief that the owner can't be discovered by taking reasonable steps.

BURGLARY

A person commits the offence of burglary when they enter any building or part of a building as a trespasser with the intent to steal, inflict grievous bodily harm, commit rape or cause unlawful damage to anything inside. To qualify as a building, the structure must be permanent with walls and a roof.

AGGRAVATED BURGLARY

The offence of aggravated burglary occurs when a person commits a burglary, but has with them at the time a firearm (including an airgun), an imitation firearm or anything that gives the appearance of being a firearm (whether or not it is capable of being fired), any other offensive weapon or any explosive.

ROBBERY

A person is guilty of robbery if they steal and, either immediately before or in the course of doing so, use force against their victim, or put them in fear of being subjected to force. A typical example would be a person who is approached in the street by someone who threatens them with a knife and forces them to hand over their wallet or handbag. It is quite common for people to tell the police that their house has been 'robbed', when what they actually mean is 'burgled'. In general, people are robbed, and buildings are burgled.

ASSAULT

An assault is any act that intentionally or recklessly causes the victim to expect immediate and unlawful personal injury or violence. An assault may occur by the use of threats, but there must be the ability to carry out those threats at the time, as words alone would not amount to an assault. An assault does not have to involve the actual application of force, which would be a battery.

COMMON ASSAULT

Common assault occurs when a person unlawfully hits or beats another. This could be a slap around the head or face, or other parts of the body. The police do not usually deal with this type of assault, and the victim may be advised to instigate proceedings for compensation, which will be held in a civil court.

ACTUAL BODILY HARM (ABH)

Actual bodily harm is defined as 'any hurt which interferes with the health or comfort, but not to a considerable degree'. This type of assault would leave physical marks, for example scratches, bruising, a black eye or a bloody nose. Bodily harm can also include psychiatric illness.

GRIEVOUS BODILY HARM (GBH)

Any person who, unlawfully and maliciously, intentionally wounds or causes grievous bodily harm to another (with or without any form of weapon) is guilty of this offence. Grievous bodily harm means any injury that is likely to take a long time to recover from, or one that will never be recovered from.

DISABILITY DISCRIMINATION ACT

This act makes it illegal to discriminate against disabled people. In the main, it applies to access to goods, facilities, services and the wider environment. It also applies when renting or buying property. BS 5619 is a voluntary code of practice for the design of housing for the convenience of disabled people.

USEFUL CONTACTS

DIRECTGOV (public service information)
www.direct.gov.uk

CROWN PROSECUTION SERVICE
www.cps.gov.uk/publications/
householders.html

CHAPTER 10

Defensive shrubs and trees

Many shrubs and small trees can be used to good effect as natural defence barriers. Careful design and the successful establishment of plants will ultimately determine the effectiveness of a defensive planting scheme. This chapter lists a range of suitable plants that have been graded according to their defensive properties, using a scale of 1 to 4, where 1 is the most effective and defensive, and 4 is the least effective.

The following plants have been selected by Writtle Agricultural College in Chelmsford, Essex. All are fairly hardy within the British Isles, and are available from most garden centres and nurseries.

Shrubs

KEY

D = Deciduous
E = Evergreen
SE = Semi-evergreen

KEY	GENUS	SPECIES	CULTIVAR	DEFENSIVE PROPERTIES	
				Grade	
D	Aralia	elata		4	Sparse, but stout, spiny stems reaching 2 m (6 ft 6 in).
	Berberis		All berberis are spiny and make excellent barrier hedges. Many of the deciduous varieties have good autumn colour, flowers and berries.		
D	Berberis group	carminea	'Buccaneer'	3	Rounded shrub to 1.2 m (4 ft).
D	Berberis	x ottawensis	'Purpurea'	3	Purple-leaved upright shrub to 1.8 m (6 ft)
D	Berberis group	carminea	'Pirate King'	2	Erect dense branches, difficult to penetrate, to 1.2 m (4 ft).
D	Berberis	thunbergii	'Atropurpurea' to 1.2 m (4 ft).	2	A vigorous, purple-leaved shrub
D	Berberis		'Red Chief'	2	Wine-coloured foliage on upright branches to 1.5 m (5 ft).
D	Berberis		'Rose Glow'	3	Mottled purple-, pink- and white-leaved shrub to 1.2 m (4 ft). Weaker than above.
SE	Berberis	wilsonae		3	A semi-evergreen, dense shrub to 1.2 m (4 ft).
E	Berberis	darwinii		2	A popular and very thorny shrub to 2 m (6 ft 6 in).
E	Berberis	gagnepainii		1	A large thorny shrub to 1.5 m (5 ft) with razor-sharp leaves.
E	Berberis	julianae		1	Long, three-armed spines and sharp leaves, to 2.7 m (9 ft).

KEY	GENUS	SPECIES	CULTIVAR	DEFENSIVE PROPERTIES	
				Grade	
E	Berberis	x stenophylla		1	Virtually impenetrable thicket of arched, spined branches to 1.8 m (6 ft).
E	Berberis	verruculosa		2	A sturdy shrub to 1.2 m (4 ft) with spiny leaves.
D	Chaenomeles	speciosa		3	A thorn-bearing shrub with red flowers that is often wall trained, to 2 m (6 ft 6 in).
E	Colletia			1	A very thorny shrub to 1.5 m (5 ft). Scented white flowers.
SE	Corokia	cotoneaster		3	A tangle of branches to 1 m (3 ft); from New Zealand.
D	Crataegus	monogyna (hawthorn)		1	A good native shrub or tree ideal for a hedge barrier.
D	Crataegus	oxycantha	'Pauls Scarlet'	2	Similar to above with double red flowers. Commonly grown as a tree.
D	Crataegus	prunifolia		1	Grown as a shrub or tree with very strong and abundant thorns.
D	Elaeagnus	angustifolia	'Oleaster'	1	A fast-growing, spiny shrub to 2 m (6 ft 6 in); scented flowers.
E	Elaeagnus	x ebbingei		2	A good evergreen forming a dense shrub to 2 m (6 ft 6 in); fragrant flowers.
E	Elaeagnus	pungens	'Maculata'	3	Less vigorous than the above, but variegated gold and green leaves.
SE	Genista	hispanica (Spanish gorse)		2 1 m	A low-growing, dense shrub to (3 ft); good yellow flowers. Prefers dry soil and sun.
SE	Genista	aetnensis (Mount Etna broom)		3	Taller, but less dense than the above. Good yellow flowers.
D	Hippophae	rhamnoides (sea buckthorn)		1	A wind- and salt-tolerant, dense shrub to 2 m (6 ft 6 in); good deterrent plant on poor soils.
E	Ilex	x altaclarensis	'Golden King'	3	Ideal for defensive hedging, with gold-edged leaves, but no berries.
E	Ilex	aquifolium (common holly)		2	The holly is native to Britain and ideal for barrier plantings; will grow to 2 m (6 ft 6 in) on most soil types.
E	Ilex	aquifolium	'Argentea Marginata'	3	A form of holly, slower growing, to 1.5 m (5 ft); good berries.

KEY	GENUS	SPECIES	CULTIVAR	DEFENSIVE PROPERTIES	
				Grade	
E	Ilex	aquifolium	'Golden Queen'	3	Despite the name, this male golden-variegated form will not produce berries.
E	Mahonia	aquifolium		3	A low-growing shrub to 1 m (3 ft) with spiny leaves.
E	Mahonia	x media	'Charity'	2	A taller hybrid with sharper leaves and better shape, to 1.5 m (5 ft).
E	Olearia	macrodonta (New Zealand holly)		3	A useful shrub for exposed sites, growing to 1.5 m (5 ft), with silver-toothed leaves and fragrant flowers
D	Poncirus	trifoliata (crown of thorns)		2	Slow-growing, impenetrable shrub to 1.8 m (6 ft); scented flowers. Prefers good, dry soil.
D	Prunus	spinosa (blackthorn)		1	An excellent, dense native shrub or small tree to 1.8 m (6 ft); sloe berries.
E	Pyracantha	angustifolia (many cultivars available)	'Orange Glow' 'Mojave'	1	A bushy, spiny shrub to 2.5 m (8 ft); good orange berries. As above, with red berries.
D	Rhamnus (buckthorn)	frangula		1	A vigorous British native shrub to 1.5 m (5 ft). Ideal for wet, peaty soils.
SE	Ribes	speciosum		3	A dense, spiny bush to 1.2 m (4 ft); fuchsia-like flowers.
D	Robinia	hispida	'Rosea'	3	Sparsely-branched, but thorny, shrub; good on walls. Pink flowers.
D	Rosa	Within the Rosa family, there are over 400 different varieties. The selection below lists the shrub varieties most suited for defensive planting. Note that some rose varieties are thornless, eg. R. 'Zephirine Drouhin' (climber). 'R' denotes a rambling rose, and 'C' denotes a climber. *See also list of top ten climbers, opposite.*			
D	R	officinalis		2	The Lancaster rose; to 1.2 m (4 ft) with red flowers.
D	R	moyesii	'Geranium'	2	A tall shrub rose to 2 m (6 ft 6 in) with pitcher-shaped hips.
D	R		'Ballerina'	3	A ground-cover rose with pink flowers.
D	R		'Dunwich Rose'	2	A very vigorous ground-cover rose with white flowers.
D	R	rugosa (many available)	'Blanc de Coubert'	2	Large white roses on very spiny stems.
D	R	rugosa	'Frau Dagmar Hastrup'.	2	As above, with pink roses

KEY	GENUS	SPECIES	CULTIVAR	DEFENSIVE PROPERTIES	
				Grade	
D	R	rugosa	'Sarah Van Fleet'	2	As above.
D	R		'Emily Gray'	2	Rich, gold, double-scented flowers; vigorous rambler, to 3 m (10 ft).
D	C	Rosa	'Guinee'	2	Scarlet fragrant flowers, to 3 m (10 ft).
D	C	Rosa	'Leaping Salmon'	2	Salmon-pink flowers, to 3 m (10 ft) and 1.8 m (6 ft) spread.
D	C	Rose	'School Girl'	2	Fragrant orange-apricot flowers, disease resistant; to 3.6 m (12 ft).
D	C	Rosa	'Allen Chandler'	2	Vigorous, dark red flowers, to 9 m (30 ft).
D	C	Rosa	'Breath of Life'	2	Apricot-pink flowers, to 2.8 m (9 ft) and 2.2 m (7 ft) spread.
D	C	Rosa	'High Hopes'	2	Pink-yellow flowers, to 3 m (10 ft) and 2.2 m (7 ft) spread.
D	Rubus	cockburnianus		1	Tall, spine covered, whitewashed stems forming a wall of thorns; very quick to establish on most soils. An excellent deterrent.
E	Ulex	europaeus	'Plenus'	1	As above, with double yellow flowers.
E	Smilax	aspera		3	A prickly climber for walls and fences; quite rare.
E	Ulex	europaeus (common gorse)		1	A superb native barrier shrub, growing to 1.5 m (5 ft). Very good on poor dry soils.

Top ten climbers

There is a vast range of hardy climbing roses. The ten climbers listed here have been selected because they are exceptionally vigorous and are suitable for growing against old trees, and for covering walls and fences. They have also been chosen for their stems, which are covered with hooked thorns.

American Pillar	Strong-growing with bright pink single flowers and dark green leaves. Ideal for training against a wall or fence; grows to 6 m (20 ft).
Compassion	Vigorous in growth with large, double, pink to apricot fragrant blooms and dark green glossy foliage throughout the summer; grows to 3 m (10 ft).
Danse du Feu	Vigorous in growth with bright orange-scarlet flowers, which repeat flowering; grows to 2.4 m (8 ft).

Iceberg	Vigorous in growth with large, pink flushed white flowers; grows to 3 m (10 ft).
Ginger Syllabub	Fragrant, golden apricot flowers; grows to 3 m (10 ft).
Golden Showers	Fragrant, pale gold flowers in summer and autumn with dark green leaves; grows to about 2.4 m (8 ft).
New Dawn	Silvery-pink flowers with dark green leaves; moderately vigorous to 3 m (10 ft). The small, fragrant double flowers are borne almost continuously throughout summer.
Wedding Day	An extremely vigorous climber that grows to 6 m (20 ft). It has yellow buds that open to deeply fragrant, almost single white flowers with prominent orange stems.
Handel	A perpetually flowering variety, suitable for a wall or pergola, with creamy-white double flowers; grows to about 3.5 m (11 ft).
Marigold	A sharply thorned climber with scented bronze and yellow double flowers that are recurrent if deadheaded; grows to 3 m (10 ft).

Trees

KEY

1. = Columnar/slender Often used for defining a boundary or providing screening, these trees can be used where foliage is necessary close to ground level, although care must be taken to choose the right tree for the right location; planting several trees close together would negate their use within the concept of 'designing out crime'.
The columnar species recommended here grow to various heights, which minimise the opportunity for concealment.

2. = Open aspect/tall trunk before branching These trees allow for clear sight lines at eye level, not only reducing the fear of crime, but also preventing concealment of potential offenders. Some pruning may be required to prevent lower branches from forming, but generally the species listed naturally develop high crowns before branching begins. Open-aspect or see-through trees, particularly those with tall trunks, allow for better natural observation than dense-foliage trees.

3. = Thorny/spiny These trees are used as a deterrent to stop anyone from climbing to gain access to your property. Many have good colour in both the spring and autumn/winter.

KEY	GENUS	SPECIES	CULTIVAR	DEFENSIVE PROPERTIES
1	Acer	platanoides	'Columnare'	A small, deciduous tree with good autumn colour, to 12 m (39 ft).
1	Acer	saccharinu	'Temples Upright' or 'Pyramidale'	A deciduous tree with very good autumn colour. Susceptible to salt damage, so avoid planting near highways; to 14 m (46 ft).
1	Carpinus	betulus	'Columnaris'	A small, narrow variety of the common hornbeam. Yellow leaves in autumn, to 10 m (33 ft).

KEY	GENUS	SPECIES	CULTIVAR	DEFENSIVE PROPERTIES
1	Populus	alba	'Raket'	A deciduous, narrow poplar reaching over 16 m (52 ft). Avoid planting near buildings due to strong, invasive roots.
1	Populus	x canadensis	'Eugenei'	A very tall poplar, reaching 30 m (98 ft). Avoid planting near buildings due to strong invasive roots.
1	Populus	nigra	'Italica' (Lombardy poplar)	A very fast-growing tree reaching 30 m (98 ft), with long male catkins. Avoid panting near buildings due to strong invasive roots.
1	Quercus	robur	'Fastigiata'	A deciduous, upright oak with dense branches reaching 16 m (52 ft).
2	Acer	henryi		A deciduous, spreading tree, to 8 m (26 ft).
2	Acer	negundo	(box elder)	A fast-growing, deciduous spreading tree, to 9 m (29 ft).
2	Acer	rubrum	'Scanlon'	A medium-sized tree forming a conical head of branches, up to 16 m (52 ft).
2	Betula	papyrifera	(paper bark birch)	A vigorous, deciduous, open-branched tree with attractive, peeling white bark; to 15 m (49 ft).
2	Betula	pendula	dalecarlica (Swedish birch)	An elegant, open-crowned deciduous tree with deeply serrated leaves, to 16 m (52 ft).
2	Betula	utilis	'Silver Shadow'	An attractive deciduous tree with striking white bark, to 12 m (39 ft).
2	Sorbus		'Joseph Rock'	A deciduous upright tree with good autumn colour and distinctive yellow berries; to 9 m (29 ft).
3	Crataegus	monogyna	(hawthorn)	A small, thorny deciduous tree, or tall hedge, of dense spreading habit, to 8 m (26 ft).
3	Crataegus	crus-galli	(cockspur thorn)	A very thorny tree, similar to hawthorn, to 8 m (26 ft).
3	Crataegus	pedicellata	(scarlet haw)	A wide spreading, dense tree with long, strong spines, to 9 m (29 ft).
3	Crataegus	prunifolia		A small, compact deciduous tree with good thorns and good autumn colour; to 8 m (26 ft).
3	Gleditsia	aquatica	(water locust)	A small shrubby tree with spiny branches and trunk, to 10 m (33 ft).
3	Gleditsia	caspica	(Caspian locust)	A small tree with formidably thorny branches and trunk, to 8 m (26 ft).
3	Gleditsia	delavayi		A rarer form of the locust tree with enormous spines, to 7 m (23 ft).
3	Gleditsia	triacanthos	(honey locust)	A very vigorous, large tree with a thorny trunk and branches, tolerates air pollution well, to 20 m (65 ft).
3	Maclura	ponifera	(osage orange)	A spiny, open-crowned tree with large unusual fruits, good on well drained chalk soils; to 8 m (26 ft).
3	Prunus	spinosa	(blackthorn/sloe)	A dense, small bushy native tree, to 8 m (26 ft).
3	Robina	pseudoacacia	(false acacia)	A fast growing, large elegant tree with spiny shoots, good on polluted sites; to 25 m (82 ft).
3	Robina	pseudoacacia	'Frisia'	A golden-leaved, small version of the above, to 10 m (33 ft).

Acknowledgements

We are indebted to Alan McInnes and Richard Childs from ACPO CPI Ltd for their permission to use the Secured by Design logo on this book and for Alan's hard work in reviewing it for accuracy. We are particularly grateful to Jon Cole of ACPO CPI Ltd for helping us with the British and European Standards. Humbled thanks goes to Julie Brennan, Terry Cocks, Pat Cogan, Andy Heasman, Steve Kong, Mick Standing, Des Rock, and Charlie Rowell from the Partnership Team at Camden Police HQ for listening to Calvin going on and on about it and helping out. Also to Paul Anstee, the Met Police Crime Prevention Manager, for putting us in touch with the publishers in the first place. Our thanks to Richard Flint of the Building Research Establishment and Steve Town from West Yorkshire Police for their help with the door and window standards. Huge gratitude goes to Writtle Agricultural College in Chelmsford, Essex, for the plant lists and thankfulness of huge order goes to Mark Whitworth from Camden Council's Planning Department for helping even though he didn't know he was. Thank you to Rosemary Wilkinson and Corinne Masciocchi and all at New Holland for wanting to do this book and trusting a couple of cops to do it. Best wishes to our old colleagues John Gridley and Tony Ashdown for working with us all those years ago on the first book that didn't quite make it. Dollops of appreciation to Alan Roberts of Merseyside Police for help with alleyway gating. A very big thank you to Inspector Dave Northcott and the High Crime Tech Unit of Essex Police for their very valued assistance. Hefty volumes of appreciation to long-suffering friends and colleagues John Hills of Essex Police, Bob Knights of AKA Training and Consultancy Ltd, Tom Webster of D W Windsor Lighting, the Brentwood District Council Environmental Health Officers and Chelmsford Borough Council Environmental Health Dept. And, of course, extraordinarily large hugs and kisses to our understanding families who supported and put up with us during the long months of penning the draft and burning the midnight oil.

Calvin Beckford and Heather Alston

Comments about this book or any new ideas for a future edition?
Please email: calvinbeckford@btconnect.com